Laila ke Khutoot

Laila ke Khutoot

The Letters of Laila

Qazi Abdul Ghaffar

Translated from Urdu
by Scheherazade Alim

NIYOGI
BOOKS

Published by
NIYOGI BOOKS
D-78, Okhla Industrial Area, Phase-I
New Delhi-110 020, INDIA
Tel: 91-11-26816301, 49327000
Fax: 91-11-26810483, 26813830
email: niyogibooks@gmail.com
website: www.niyogibooksindia.com

Editor: Shiny Das/Niyogi Books
Cover Design: Arati Devasher
Layout: Shashi Bhushan Prasad/Niyogi Books

ISBN: 978-93-83098-08-8
Publication: 2013

Other than actual historical persons and events, portrayed according to the author's interpretation, all characters appearing in this book are a work of the author's imagination. Any resemblance to actual persons is entirely coincidental.

Printed at: Niyogi Offset Pvt. Ltd., New Delhi, India

To the memory of
the late Professor S. Mujtaba Hussain
who first introduced me to this work

Contents

Translator's Note

I first made Laila's acquaintance in the course of studying Urdu literature many years ago. This translation has been a stimulating and rewarding re-introduction. The work falls into two parts. The first part is *Laila ke Khutoot,* the Letters of Laila and the second part is *Majnun ki Diary*. The author has in each case written detailed explanatory comments setting out his aims and objectives and I have included these comments in their entirety. They are most illuminating.

My warmest thanks to Professor M.S.Z. Chaghtai, former Head of the Department of Physics, Aligarh Muslim University, for generously giving me his time and for dealing meticulously with the various points that I raised. I have tried to convey the flavour and sense of the work, and have tried, wherever possible, to find the appropriate English idiom whilst doing my best not to depart too far from the text.

Any shortcomings and errors are mine alone.

Scheherazade Alim

Aligarh, May 2007

Qazi Abdul Ghaffar

Qazi Abdul Ghaffar was a respected and well-known name in Urdu literary circles in India in the first half of the twentieth century. He was a distinguished journalist, essayist and a man of letters. The modernity, frankness, and open-mindedness revealed both in *Laila ke Khutoot* and *Majnun ki Diary* reflect Qazi Abdul Ghaffar's own nature. Opinions (even in his family) differ about the exact year of his birth. On his death in 1954 his age was given as sixty-six years by some papers, and as sixty-eight years by others. A safe assumption appears to be that he was born between 1888 and 1889 into a distinguished and deeply religious family of Moradabad. His formal education does not appear to have been extensive. Initially he was educated at the English Middle School in Moradabad, and in 1910 came to the Mohammedan Anglo-Oriental College, Aligarh (this became the Aligarh Muslim University in 1920) to do his FA (Intermediate). Despite two attempts to pass he was not successful and thereafter embarked upon a career in journalism. He settled in Hyderabad, and edited an Urdu paper called *Payaam* (the message). The name was inspired by Maulana Azad's journal *Paighaam*. His literary and intellectual activities brought him into contact with the outstanding liberal minds of the time, in particular, Maulana Azad and Hakim Ajmal Khan.

Qazi Abdul Ghaffar's views were far removed from those of his deeply religious family. On a personal level Qazi Abdul Ghaffar's life was marked by tragedy. His marriage to his cousin Afzaal Begum in 1910 resulted in six children, the eldest being his daughter Zohra, followed by four sons and a daughter. His wife died a week after the birth of his younger daughter Fatima. All his sons were mentally challenged and none lived beyond the age of eighteen years. Zohra Begum was married into a landowning family and her husband Chaudhry Sultan was a professor in the Department of Political History at the Aligarh Muslim University. Deprived of her mother since birth, Fatima was adopted by her maternal uncle Sir Mohammad Yaqoob, a distinguished lawyer of Moradabad. She subsequently married Alam Ali Khan and moved to Hyderabad where she still resides. She is the only surviving child of Qazi Abdul Ghaffar.

The loss of his wife was very painful and left Qazi Abdul Ghaffar lonely and bereft. He had always been passionately fond of music, and this drew him to a circle of musicians and performers. There he met and fell in love with a courtesan called Munni Jaan who was a member of a musical troupe. Munni Jaan was originally a Hindu from the hill areas of Kumaon in U.P. but subsequently embraced Islam and took the name Sakina Begum. In 1928 Sakina Begum and Qazi Abdul Ghaffar were married in Moradabad. There being no children of this marriage, Qazi Abdul Ghaffar adopted the younger son of his eldest daughter and brought him up as his own child. Sakina Begum was a devoted wife and a great companion to Qazi Abdul Ghaffar till the end of his life, but not surprisingly Qazi Abdul Ghaffar's family did not take kindly to this marriage, and maintained no contact of any kind with Sakina Begum.

Being someone of liberal and enlightened views, (as is evident both from *Laila ke Khutoot* and *Majnun ki Diary*) Qazi Abdul Ghaffar took up his pen to crusade against the narrow mindedness and hypocrisy he saw around him. Religion for him was an entirely personal matter and he was deeply concerned about the oppression of women and their humiliation at the hands of orthodox maulvis. Like many intellectuals of the time, he felt that the Russian Revolution was a liberating, progressive event and from the very beginning he supported the Progressive Writers' Movement. In 1945 Qazi Abdul Ghaffar inaugurated the conference of progressive writers in Hyderabad, presiding over its various sessions.

During the tumult that resulted from Partition in 1947 Qazi Abdul Ghaffar was called to Delhi by Maulana Azad. At Maulana Azad's insistence, he was appointed general secretary of the Anjuman-e-Taraqqi-e-Urdu (the society for the advancement of Urdu). The offices of this body were moved from Delhi to Aligarh and Qazi Abdul Ghaffar came to live in Aligarh in an effort to secure a reasonable future for the Urdu language. He campaigned tirelessly to obtain for Urdu what he considered to be its rightful entitlements. Unfortunately, the authorities concerned were not responsive to his suggestions. It was a losing battle and the pressure took its toll on Qazi Abdul Ghaffar's health. For the last few years of his life he was continually ill—the illness was eventually diagnosed as cancer. On 17 January 1954 Qazi Abdul Ghaffar died a deeply disappointed man. He is buried in the university graveyard at Aligarh.

Laila ke Khutoot, the first edition of which was published in Hyderabad in 1934 is widely acknowledged to be Qazi Abdul Ghaffar's masterpiece. It is a graphic example of the distance which Urdu prose had travelled from the early years of the twentieth century. Its subject is in itself, little short of sensational. That the protagonist should be not only a woman but also a courtesan, was indeed something revolutionary at the time of its publication. In the early part of the twentieth century, Woman had been projected in idealised terms. She was not so much flesh and blood as a symbol of beauty and chaste affection—put on a pedestal and worshipped from afar. The achievement of Qazi Abdul Ghaffar is that he brought that idealised symbol to life. Laila is a living being, with a mind of her own and a heart full of compassion for women forced by circumstances (as she was) to adopt prostitution as a profession. Through the letters (there are fifty-two in all and they are of varying length) we get a glimpse of the daily life of a courtesan. The throng of her admirers from all walks of life is vividly described; they come from all sections of society and are in pursuit of sensual pleasures. The letters are by turn witty, philosophical and deeply moving. Even in the company of her Majnun, Laila maintains her individuality with humour and skill. She is never subservient to him. Despite her bitter, sordid and sad life, Laila yet manages to retain an innate innocence. She is a person whose thoughts we share and who elicits our sympathy. Needless to say, the publication of this book caused a furore at that time. The sympathetic and understanding portrayal of the life of a prostitute completely devoid of any moral starchiness, the refreshing frankness with which she speaks about sensuality and the physical relations between men and women, was something which had never been dealt with before. The oppression and humiliation which the life of a courtesan entails is described most eloquently and with great feeling. Laila demands for justice—her complaint is that the whole of society has become deaf and dumb. She has been forced into prostitution, and no one is prepared to give her a hearing but the person responsible for her ruin, is an admired pillar of society!

To present the other side of the story of *Laila ke Khutoot*, Qazi Abdul Ghaffar wrote *Majnun ki Diary*. This was published in

1934. In his lengthy introduction, Qazi Abdul Ghaffar explains the rationale behind this exercise. He attempts to portray the confusion, cynicism, alienation, and sensuality of the so-called educated young men of that time who, scorning established values were adrift and saw in unbridled sensuality a panacea for their problems.

There are certain similarities in the facts between *Laila ke Khutoot* and *Majnun ki Diary*. Like Laila the protagonist of *Laila ke Khutoot*, the Bi Laila of Majnun's Diary also leaves town and seeks refuge elsewhere and nurses Manjun but in conception, Bi Laila is not Laila's equal. She is a lesser creation and does not elicit our sympathy to the extent that Laila does. Though entertaining, Majnun himself seems to be more a collection of attitudes than a rounded human being. He is forever lecturing his friends on the absurdity of religion, of marriage, and poking fun at every norm which does not coincide with his thinking. He is not someone with whom we can easily sympathise—he is indolent, selfish, arrogant, and totally confused. Despite the fact that *Majnun ki Diary* is an interesting and stimulating exercise, it is *Laila ke Khutoot* for which Qazi Abdul Ghaffar will be remembered and which is his enduring literary contribution.

Abba ki Baat (About Abba)

Qazi Abdul Ghaffar's younger daughter, Begum Fatima Alam Ali Khan brings her father to life in this charming essay. Below are extracts translated from that essay.

Abba very seldom laughed loudly. Sometimes, if he ever guffawed, he would control himself so quickly that it seemed as if by laughing loudly he had done something seriously wrong. He loved good food and dressing well, and always dressed in the height of fashionable good taste. He usually wore *churidars* and a matching cap on his head and when he went out in his elegantly tailored *sherwani* I always whispered a prayer for him, to keep away evil beings. He always used to say to me, 'Please learn to hold your tongue; otherwise you'll have a bad time with your in-laws.' Goodness knows how many hearts he must have conquered with his winning ways, but of course he was not going to tell us. The element of thrift did not exist in Abba's life. I can honestly say that whatever he earned, he spent in entertaining his friends. He never bothered with any form of accounting, and was notoriously inaccurate with figures. He was never concerned by how much he earned as the editor of *Payaam* or with keeping an account of household expenses. 'What on earth is the use of keeping an account of money which has already been spent?' he would ask.

Apart from his books and pencils, which were as precious to him as life itself, Abba was notoriously forgetful about things.

At times, he would put his pencil into his mouth instead of his cigarette, and would constantly try to light it with no success! Whoever was with him on such occasions, would point out to him that there was no cigarette but a pencil in his month. He would then roar with laughter. The same thing used to happen with his spectacles. He would be wearing them, yet forgetting that, would frantically look for them turning everything upside down.

When I came to stay with Abba, *Payaam* was at the height of its fame. All week he would be involved in setting the paper. Having finished this task, he would come home, completely preoccupied. One could see the articles taking shape in his head. He was so involved in his world that he was not aware of who was around him or what was going on. For instance, on one occasion during dinner, I passed a plate of kebabs to him saying, 'Have some kebabs; they are delicious.' He awoke as if from a trance, and said, 'Good heavens my dear I am too busy.' The task of reminding him that he was not at his desk but at the dining table fell to me. When I whispered these words in his ear, his face would light up, he would curse his forgetfulness, and turn his attention to the food before him.

Abba very seldom got annoyed with the servants, but woe betide any servant who in any way failed to look after his dogs. The angrier Abba was, the more courteously he spoke. As a general rule, Abba got angry very seldom. If anything upset him at home or at his work, he would simply become silent, and start to tidy and dust his books and his papers. Whenever we saw him putting his papers and his books in order, we would whisper, 'Abba is in a bad mood' and a hush would descend on the whole house. Usually, Abba's anger had a fixed duration. By the third day it would evaporate and he would be his normal self again. It was only then that life returned to the house.

One day I found Abba conversing with pigeons in the garden. A female pigeon was sitting in his lap and her mate was pecking furiously at Abba's feet. We asked Abba what was going on. 'I have for several days been watching this wretched fellow,' he answered. 'The moment the cage is opened, he flies out to have the first go at the birdseed, but if the poor female tries to come out of her cage he prances in front of her and pecks her back into the cage. She, poor thing, never manages to get enough to eat.' Turning to the male pigeon he continued, 'Until I see you well and truly humbled and contrite, I will not release the female pigeon. Undoubtedly you come from a family of maulvis.' We never realised that there could be a maulvi even among pigeons!

How Abba disliked maulvis who prated about women and speechified about women's obligations to their husbands. He used to say, 'These wretched people have denied woman her rightful place.'

Laila ke Khutoot

The Letters of Laila

Preamble by the Author

These pages are self-explanatory. A small mirror has been placed before the renowned reformers and leaders of our community so that in it they can see the loathsome visage of their conventional delusions about women.

It will be grossly unfair to me if these pages are considered and read as a novel or a story. The truth is that enclosed within this fragile papery apparel is an attempt to portray some aspects of a woman's life. If people are able to understand the meaning of these sketches, so much the better, but they should also be aware that until full justice is done to women the claim of political independence and national advancement will remain an empty one!

I cannot say that this portrayal of the public and private life of a courtesan is entirely without exaggeration but I will say this that in an environment where beauty is for sale, this is a study of woman's wounded nature, which deserves to be taken as a warning by knowledgeable circles in the Urdu language and in individual and social life. This distressing portrait had to be painted in graphic colours to bring it before the eyes of the readers more vividly:

It matters not how often the truth is discussed
Unless it is presented in appropriate terms any discussion is without effect.

This collection of Laila's letters is neither a literary exercise nor a show of penmanship; in fact, those who are discerning will find that the smile Laila wears is a fountain spouting blood; her confident tone is but an entreaty, and her humour is a cry of pain. Her heart's anguish is hidden in her high spirits, and her playfulness hides her wounds. Laila's philosophy of life is in fact not so sordid as full of sadness. She plays laughingly with her wounds which have become a running sore on her existence. In her brief story Laila is in fact recounting the stories of hundreds of thousands of her unfortunate sisters who in this country are sacrificed to the lust and sensuality of men. Every aspect of Laila's life is a plea.

In substance these letters reveal some indications on the part of the oppressed to the oppressor, but oppressors always shy away from looking at any portrait of the oppressed, because the oppressed is a mirror in which the oppressor sees his real face. Small wonder then that in various circles these letters have been severely criticised. But in the world of women—where almost half the population is still in chains and is voiceless—I am hopeful that most of these pages will be read attentively.

Various letters on the same theme have already been published. In this way, some part of Laila's entreaty has reached sympathisers. I know that in certain circles this plea has been heard with sympathy. Now, the object of publishing these letters together is that those who are truly concerned about Laila should extract a drop of blood from their individual and collective lives and they should put this drop under a microscope to find all the bacteria which are eating away at our way of life. Laila, in reality, is only a single a drop of blood which I wish to put before the revered elders of our community. Instead of sitting on prayer mats with a *tasbih* and mouthing irrelevant, pious platitudes from mosques, these worthies should devise a healing balm for this running sore in their culture of which Laila is but one drop of blood. If only these worthies did not think it sufficient leadership merely to deliver speeches from platforms in an attempt to bring solace to the victims!

Abdul Ghaffar
04.12.1932

This humble tribute is offered by a fallen sister to those of her sisters who are fortunate and respected, and who have been spared her anguish and her wounds.

The first letter

Your few lines are concise, but not beyond my comprehension. Your letter is not the first of its kind in my life! For many years, I have been spending the greater part of my days and nights writing such letters. The life which I am now leading is no longer new to me—why do you try to hide a guilty conscience behind a screen of words? There is no scope here for shame or inhibition. The difficulty is simply that you wish to create a conventional pattern for our relationship. Why don't you frankly say that you are also a purchaser of my attractions? You have confessed that my company at night is a source of delight to you. Why don't you also admit that you are looking for something beyond mere physical intimacy? Is that not the case? My friend, if you go shopping, avoid metaphors and oblique references, and strike a bargain clearly and openly as any purchaser does. You will tell me that in your letter you have preserved all the courtesies, decorum, and restraint, but what is the use of these contrivances in my case? If you wish me to spend this evening with you, what excuse can I have for not doing so? This is why I publicly advertise my charms.

The second letter

My most gracious friend! Thank you for everything that made last night so pleasant. And thank you also for thinking of me.

Why do you waste your demonstrations of regard on an unworthy creature like myself? It is not at all necessary that the delights of the evening which is past should exist the next morning. You should remain where you are and let me remain where I am. It is best that way.

The third letter

My valued admirer! How long ago was it that I was your guest and how long has it been since you began showering your youthful ardour on me? How often have I told you not to go beyond the limits of what is possible: Do not ask for what cannot be.

Yesterday evening you expressed your feelings of affection amidst hot tears and strangled sobs. I was, as a result, quite exhausted. How can I make you understand that this kind of emotional outburst does not affect me one little bit? My femininity and feminine charms are openly on sale and are purchased by the public. This is the trade which I carry on but you refuse to accept this reality, and hurtful though it may be, it still is *reality*. This unrealistic attitude of yours will come up time and again and my answer will be the same as before. There is no other answer that I can give you. It is impossible for me to come today. Tomorrow, or the day after, should you so desire, I will certainly come but you must promise that you will not pester me with poetic and fanciful thoughts. You are like a child running after an unreal object and when the object cannot be obtained, you create a scene. Dear friend, the point at which you and I have arrived, is in fact our journey's end. Beyond this point, our paths diverge. So don't push matters too far and I will come with you as far as I can. Thereafter, if you wish to go on any further, you must travel alone.

The fourth letter

You must be waiting, lost in fanciful thought. If I were to tell you the reason for not going, you will say, 'How hard-hearted this woman is!' But what can I do? I am not in the habit of discreetly sidestepping issues. From the very beginning I have tried to make you see matters in their true light. Understand that black is black and not otherwise, and see the blemishes on my raiment with your own eyes. Do not be deceived by my feminine allure. This is only an advertisement. You have more humanity in you than I do, and even though I do not love you, I am a sincere well-wisher. You have only just set foot in the real world and are not yet acquainted with the ups and downs of life. Let others be deceived. So far as I am concerned, even if I lose you, there will still be plenty of fools in the world.

My precious friend! Even though I am quite indifferent to your displays of affection and will always be so—do not think that I find no pleasure in your embrace. It is my destiny and not my temperament which is bad. My life is deeply blemished, but before I entered this flesh trade, I was fortunate enough to have had a grounding in education, culture and decency, far in excess of those generally possessed by wives and daughters-in-law of respected families. Don't regard this statement of mine as being an exercise in self-deception and conceit. I too once possessed potential—providence did give me my share, but my life has made my soul bitter and empty. In my heart of hearts I am ashamed of my existence; I have been thrown into the dirt by this loathsome world and its most loathsome inhabitants and now I am stuck in this filth. Heavy, sinful fetters bind my feet. But despite this, something of beauty and grace still survives. If it were not so, I would not be able to talk to you as I am doing. When you are tired of demonstrating your affection, of making lengthy declarations of love and hear not a word of love from me in return, then what foolish questions you ask me! Sometimes you say, 'Laila, you are angry', or 'Can my love never be requited?', 'You are so hard-hearted!', or 'You are so uncaring, so insensitive, there is no harmony in any part of you, you are an iceberg, a heavy stone, a lifeless portrait—you are a river whose water is frozen and immovable. Why are you like this?' Then you recall my present life and putting your arm around my neck you say, 'Are you like this with your other admirers? Have you never experienced the joy of love? Has that fortunate man not been born whom you can love with all your heart?'

How many nights have you wasted in this way my valued friend! You are searching for life in a wilderness, for an oasis in a desert. You require your love to be shared by an understanding and intimate companion. I cannot fulfil these requirements. Yes, I can give you an attractive body to clasp in your arms, a pretty face for you to embrace, I can spread my perfumed hair in your lap. But this is my limit. Please do not ask for or desire anything beyond this.

One day when you were repeatedly asking me why I am like this, perhaps I promised that I would tell you, if it were possible to do so, why I became like I am. During this period of time, there have been many occasions when as a result of your unrealistic fancies I have reproached myself and thought that I would then tell you a story. But my heart warned me that you are a young man not yet in a settled frame of mind. I thought I would wait until your passion was spent and you were in control of your emotions. When I look at you I see that you do not stand firmly on this treacherous and slippery ground. What you think is a stormy ocean is in fact a filthy pond, which is shallow and which you could have waded across without difficulty. But what can I do in the face of your illusions—you consider yourself to be standing on the shore of a boundless ocean, although let me tell you a storm-tossed ocean and a small pond have the same reality. It all depends upon how you look at it—the stormy ocean and the still pond are all a delusion. If you imagine it to be so, an ocean will seem to be a pond, and a pond an ocean. Once fancy takes root in the mind that is the truth and all the rest is beside the point. In your mind there is both the ocean and the pond, and in reality both are the same, but when you close your eyes and insist that a pond is in truth an ocean, then every drop of water will have the quality of a tempest for you. You must have seen plenty of *hakims* and philosophers. I am a philosopher whose attractions are for sale.

The potter makes a pretty earthen vessel. People regard it as a cup for drinking wine. The potter makes a cup for drinking wine and people think it is an earthen vessel for holding water and they put it on the wall of the mosque. Does this alter the reality of the earth from which the vessel has been made? You can put either wine or the *Zamzam* in a drinking vessel—a woman can have the status of a servant or the queen of the house—whatever you wish. Men have made woman serve them in whatever image they have wanted; they have made her a slave, they have made her serve their carnal desires, they have put her in the market for sale. You have robbed the diamond of its sparkle and whatever little was left, you have trampled in the dust; you have robbed the pearl of its lustre and thrown what was left to blow away in the breeze. What now remains to give any meaning to your tales of love?

You must be tired of this nonsense, but there is a meaning behind my words. If you are able to grasp the meaning, do so, and learn a little wisdom from me. I am free this evening. When I am alone and free from my hordes of admirers, (Alas my bed is very rarely free of these wretched people!) I lie down and forget all my admirers and their protestations of love—for a little while it is my particular occupation to fancy myself in the guise of a lover and I make my real self my beloved. It is as if I am someone else whose head is in my lap and to whom I say, 'Laila ... wretched unfortunate Laila. Are you free today? Is it a holiday? Are you tired? Are you searching for something? Are you thinking of someone? This night is an empty one. Go to sleep. Tomorrow you will again have to open your shop. Purchasers will come and bargains will be struck. Take your fate in your hands and go to sleep.'

The fifth letter

I am thankful that you have promised to restrain your impatience and restlessness. I will visit you this evening. When it rains, sensible people keep not one but two umbrellas. In case one gets lost, the other comes in useful. Sensible men too, do not select just one woman to be their plaything and the sole recipient of their ardour. They keep several women so that their evenings are not wasted. When I am too busy to visit you, you spend the entire night sulking and being out of sorts. If only you had made alternative arrangements, your night would not have been empty without my presence. I entreat you not to bestow your attentions on a woman whose affections are for sale. There should be more than one arrow in your quiver. Look at me, who like a gilded butterfly flits from one garden to another; I commune with each flower upon which I alight. Like the honeybee you too should go from flower to flower, spending a few moments to savour the pleasures of each. Why from morn till night do you remain fixated by my outlook on life? My words hide a dry, bitter reality. Despite that, look at the way I keep my cup brimming over. It is not a satisfying draught. I am a cup full of intoxicating spirit. I fill my cup alone, but nevertheless give cheer to many who drink from it. You too should appear in company, like a cup which is full, or else forsake my company.

There was a time (alas it will never return!) when I used to read with interest the stories of *Laila* and *Majnun*, *Shirin* and *Farhad*. In those days of innocence, how I used to dream of reckless rapture. But I found out that the sheer business of living does not leave time for such leisure. When life is based on a few mouthfuls of food, when one's priorities are good food and decorative raiment, when it is the body that is adorned and not the soul, then leisure is not an option.

Oh to sit and be lost in contemplation of one's beloved ...

You are not subject to the sordid pressures of life, you are confident of life and of your physical powers, you have no worries about society, you are not required to do anything for economic necessity. From morning till night, your time is your own. You are free to dream of *Laila* and *Majnun*. A good digestion, a robust constitution and a red-blooded healthy body will ensure you a pleasant existence. Look at me. I have to say that I have not adopted a profession, but the profession has adopted me.

I have not come of my own volition;
I have been brought to this pass.

So why on earth should I waste my time digressing? Then I tell myself that a woman's beauty needs to be revealed. Even a hunter kills a deer to revel in his power over the hapless creature and delight his spirit. So don't be downcast. There are plenty of flowers in this garden.

I am aware that you think of me as an insensitive and shameless woman. My dear Quais your Laila is neither insensitive nor shameless, but merely a creature forced by this deceitful world to work in order to keep body and soul together. If she were to spend her time thinking about shame and sensitivity, how would she live? If she were to allow herself to be influenced by your strictures on morality and virtue, this world would not allow her either to live or to die. At least there is the consolation that sinful though my world is, I do not have to worry about carping criticism. You with your notions of love and attachment raise the issues of moral virtue and reformed behaviour and like a deceitful *Sufi* seek to bridge the gap between illusion and reality, when all you are doing is weaving a spider's web. This is an idiotic notion and I regard it as a very bad jest. You consider our relationship as something divine and I only know that you are but one of the many purchasers who come to buy what I have to sell.

How unrealistic you are! A woman like me could have entangled you in a thousand webs. But if you think that a fish can exist on dry land, or a deer can make its home in the water, or a tiger live on the tree tops, you are much mistaken. A fish will always be a fish, a deer will always be a deer, a tiger will always remain a tiger. If you were to go to a wine house and ask for water to perform ritual ablutions before prayers or if you were to sit in a mosque and pour yourself a glass of wine from a decanter, what would the world say? How topsy turvy your thinking is!

The sixth letter

My caring lover! You ask me why last night I cried in your arms. You were so amazed by my crying! As if for you my eyes were incapable of tears. Like an innocent player who picks up a *sitar* in a gathering and attempts to play it but does not know how to play and then when his untrained fingers touch one of the strings of the sitar, the player wonders how the string has produced such a sound. He wonders why the sound is not the sound he had imagined. Because the player is unskilled, he does not understand the technique of playing the *sitar*, and how the strings are to be plucked. So he clumsily hits the strings and complains that no melodious tune issues from the instrument. Only noise is produced. This untrained, unskilled player has no idea of the strings of the *sitar* or the music they can produce. He has no idea which string he is touching or what its sound should be. How can you know the number of strings which my silent *sitar* has? When some untrained player chances to touch a string, suddenly a helpless musical note fills the air like a shriek and the untrained player does not know—he cannot know—where this melodious harmony has come from. How can you know that in a woman's tears there exists a world of music? Oh, you who are in raptures on seeing the cosmetic redness of my eyes, how can you ever find the music in my tears? ... this is my secret.

A woman is brimming with the music and poetry of life. Are you even aware of this fact? My dear friend, you are like an ignorant nurse who, not knowing how many wounds the sheet on a wounded patient's body covers or where the wounds are, touches the wounded body wherever he likes. When the patient cries out in pain, the nurse is amazed and wonders why the patient has cried out. You have no idea which of my wounds you put your finger on and what you are doing, and if, when my pain and hurt become uncontrollable, I cry out, you ask me why I am crying. You have no idea that you are playing with the strings of my wounded heart! Like you, many men play, and in the course of their playing know not how many strings they break, whose music is stilled forever. Perhaps there now remains only a single string which is unbroken. Do not search for this, lest your insensitive fingers wish to play with this string also. Heavens above! What vistas of buffoonery have opened up for you as a result of my tears! You ask, 'Are you in economic difficulties? Does the memory of anyone disturb you?' You may consider my tears as a feminine contrivance but explain to the uncontrolled beast, which is in you and which is in every man, that for a man, a woman's tears have an intoxicating quality, that women should sometimes shed tears so that their tears too become a means of adding further allure and can be a source of joy in the sensual world. A man is constantly demanding a new technique from a woman and considers a heightened level of sensuality to be sufficient. A man gets tired of a woman who always smiles, or is always in tears. He desires every condition to be transient to enhance his sensual pleasure. The beast in every man wants to hold in his hand the cup, which instead of wine, is filled with a woman's blood so that he may remain intoxicated.

Oh you unthinking man! How painful and difficult for you will be those moments when your intoxication begins to wear off!

The seventh letter

You are unacquainted with pain! Why do you insist on deceiving yourself? Your heart continues to be rash and intemperate. Your protestations of love echo in the air, as if apart from your love and my beauty there is nothing else on earth, as if these two things are enough by themselves to gain the universe!

You are under the impression that you are perhaps the first man who has been in love with me, who has prostrated himself at the altar of my beauty. Sometime or other I will tell you what a remarkable array of lovers come to see me every day, who, in the stakes of love, are miles ahead of you. To this list I have also added your name. What more do you want? I realise that you are a faithful and true lover of mine, but find it most unreasonable that you should also want to be my beloved. Although an admirer may not admit the fact in so many words, every admirer's desire is that his affection be reciprocated in the same way. Why should this be? When did your beloved ever entreat you to give her the pleasure of your company and start bestowing your affection on her? If you feel you have no choice but to love me, well in God's name do so as ardently as you can. But what peculiar logic is it that just because you are madly in love, your beloved should also be in love with you? Listen my valued friend, I respect your plain speaking. Love is the elixir of life. It is impossible to describe! If you are capable of ardent, sincere affection, you are to be congratulated, but why do you expect me to love you at your mere request? It is as if you had said to me 'love me' and that very instant I started to love you, and mutual love between us came into being. How extraordinary! If one were to eat somewhere outside and say to the cook, 'You eat also'—just imagine what would happen if the cook from morning till night started to eat with every customer! Severe indigestion would be the result. Every customer who comes would eat his fill and move on. But the cook for his part would have gastric problems and struggle all his life to make ends meet.

To this day I cannot understand the reason for your complaints. When I visit you, do I not spend hours in your arms? When you kiss me, do I not respond? When you pour out your heart to me, do I not listen with due concentration? The whole trouble is that you think bronze is real gold—I tell you that I am not what you think I am! You just do not believe me. When I bare my sinful life to you, all you do is close your eyes. I show you the shameful blemishes on my existence and you refuse to look! You display your unbounded restlessness and helplessness before me and drive me to distraction! You taunt me and say I have no heart, that my sinful life has made me insensitive. Your attitude is extraordinary. By this I mean that you think a flower, which is a companion of the morning breeze, has been nourished in poisoned earth. You are mistaken. It is neither the fault of the flower, nor of the earth. This flower has had the same nourishment that every others flower gets. It was born in the same earth as every other flower but some flower-gatherer in collaboration with a thief had the flower plucked from its bush and thrown around the neck of a sinful throng so that the innocent flower could be bruised and crushed by their sordid desires.

The world is full of brazen, ruthless, and poisonous persons who in order to satisfy their lust are always ready to strangle a woman. You men have made our lives—the lives of us women—bitter and ruined as if we were created merely to satisfy your desires and our own material comforts. Thousands, nay millions of women who were meant by God to be the light and adornment of their homes, who were meant to be the solace of hearts, the comfort of the confused and a support for tired travellers—it is you, men, who have thrown them into the wrong path of life! Does a woman's nature crave sinfulness? She never even takes one step towards sensuality. But like a beast of prey, a man's lust constantly lies in wait for her. When the doe is unaware of danger, this beast attacks. Then like a dove which has just escaped the clutches of an eagle, this oppressed child of God tries to hide her wounds, but she cannot hide them—she falls into disgrace and by slow degrees, gets used to her disgrace ... there are many many such wounded people in the world I inhabit. You are in a world where there are many such robbers and predators. If you cannot ask your conscience, then ask us what you do. We are the living examples of your assault and plunder. A woman is by nature innocent. It is your nature which is brimming with sinfulness. I want to ask you to tell me truthfully that when you hold me in your arms are you even aware how truly beautiful my femininity is? Or are you simply satisfying your needs? Does it ever occur to you that this toy with which your wealth is playing, was once, not a toy, but a gilded and entrancing portrait? If you break this toy, if you plunder any rights this toy may have, how is the poor toy at fault? Why do you vent your anger on it? Why do you taunt it? How many women are there who take the first step towards a man of their own accord, who have opened their arms to embrace a man? Even a virgin who has been nurtured in a sinful environment, even that wretched, shameless unfortunate woman will not call you to her and say, 'Come, and do what you wish with me.' It is you men who have put a price on her body. It is your lust which makes you desire her. You crush her spirit by your brute force and the strength of your gold and silver! When you reach out insistently towards me, why don't you ask your unquenchable lust whether this woman who offers the most precious jewel of her femininity, could have been the light of some household and whether her lap could have reared a generation of humanity! This evening such a woman adorns your bed, and tomorrow morning in the public gaze you will not even want to glance in her direction. The fact of the matter is that a man knows well how to deceive his conscience. He hides his sinful desires behind a bright and alluring façade. He calls his lust, love. He swears by this love and forces his heart and mind to be numbed by strong liquor. He says to others, 'I am in love, I am a victim of a deceiving woman, I am wronged and I am pure.' But all this posturing of love is in fact an aspect of sensuality which you show us. You cannot escape our long suffering natures. If only you could be protected from your self-deception! Step aside one instant from your sensuality-driven existence and pay heed to my request. You keep requesting me to tell you something about myself. You will find this story of mine tasteless. It will spoil the pleasure of your sensual experience. Like millions of my unfortunate sisters:

> *I am the voice of my own despair*

Where do you have the time from your protestations of love to listen to my story? I am a ruined portrait of life, which desires that you should bestow a glance and take heed of it!

The eighth letter

Well this is a new development. May God preserve you from evil eyes! You are now making scathing comments at me! Laila's Majnun! If I can find them in some bazaar, I'll buy you a *tola* or two of brains. It avails me nothing, in your eyes, to tell you the truth, and makes my leisure and tranquility meaningless. How thoughtless and wrong you are when you say,

> *What would the bird singing unharmed know of the anguish of the nightingale which the serpent has devoured under the bough.*

What you have offered me I throw back in your face.

In your entire vocabulary is there such a word as 'serpent'? If you don't know this, I'll tell you. I too have a serpent, which is coiled around my jugular vein, but the difference is that your serpent is but an aspect of your lust which keeps devouring you by slow degrees, and my serpent demands to be fed twice every day. You call me unharmed! You should die of shame for these words. You short-sighted man! The sharp-eyed falcon knows that my serpent is much deadlier than yours. Had I wanted to, I would have replied to that serpent coiled around the branch of the rose as follows:

O pigeon perched on the summit of the mosque
What would you know of the state of the hearts of the birds which flutter below?

But what can I write to you? I know very well that you understand neither the nightingale which the snake has devoured below the bough, nor the fluttering hearts of the birds. Your perverse mentality and lack of understanding make me laugh and cry. You are regarded as a mature educated young man and yet you have no more perception than a child! I am not yet twenty-five but I have been starved of all the blessings of youth. People see that I am in the bloom of youth but they don't realise that I do not find a spark of youth within myself. Beneath this beautiful rose- coloured skin lies a worn-out, wrinkled old body whose ugliness lies hidden. How cold and joyless is the hearth of my life. If only you were not a twenty-two-year-old innocent man and I were not an old woman of twenty-five! If you and I can change places then let us do so for a few days, you take my place and let me take yours. Then you will forget your youth!

Your childish naiveté is also proved by the fact that because you have not been able to get round me, you have resorted to taunts. You are unable to read even one page of the story of a woman's life. Today I will make a wager with you and show you a scene from my life. Just exchange your protestations of affection for a few hours with any evening or any day of my life. For a few moments give me all the pleasures of your life and take from me my wounds and anguish of spirit. Then see whose serpent is more poisonous, and whose wounds are deeper.

I will relate to you just one example of what I go through every day of my life. Then I will ask you whether you would ever be able to crush your heart, your mind, all the aspects of your being and your spirit into dust as I have had to do.

Like countless nights of my life, yesterday evening was just another night when I found myself in a stranger's embrace. The only reason that happened was because he had paid a heavy price for my beautiful body. In what exaggerated manner he expressed his affection for me that evening! I responded in kind. I struggled with the realisation that this stranger would all at once declare his ardour and want all the delights of my body to be sacrificed to his sensuality. I knew that perhaps the next morning he and I would never be united, but he had paid heavily for the few hours of night and I had to give him value for his money so I had to endure his embrace with a smile. You will never believe how spontaneously I laughed at his words. The whole room resounded with my laughter. He expressed his sensual pleasure in the most vulgar and coarse terms and I tried to make him happy by praising his disgusting and vulgar words. All evening, at every stage, I was a perfect match to him.

When I came home in the morning, I was exhausted, my eyes were sore with lack of sleep, my heart was sore, my spirits were low, and my mind was worried. All I wanted to do was to snatch some sleep and forget all about the wretched evening that had passed. I was just planning to go to bed and the wilted, jaded flowers of yesterday were still round my neck when I heard a movement and collected my wits. The person who was there was one of my most ardent admirers. He had brought with him a long tale of his love. He always comes in this manner. He kept staring at me, then took my hand in his and started to squeeze my hand in an attempt to transfer some of the current of his desire to my body. Then his hand reached my neck, his head touched my head. His warm breath stank. In it were mixed the stench of pyorrhoea and flavoured tobacco, and hit my cheeks like a hot pestilential wind. Finally, after a lengthy preamble of his affection, he came to the point, by saying to me, 'Please come and visit me tonight.' There was no lack on my part in expressing my affection. On such occasions I always conceal my real face beneath a professional mask and put on a face which is smiling, resplendent and full of vitality and strength. He had also brought for me a beautiful present and after that, his words—'do visit me tonight'—meant that he had already paid for my services. At long last thank God he left and I put my head upon my pillow. I was not quite asleep when a maid came with a letter. This was also a message of love, together with the entreaty, 'Please do come tonight.' I sat up and replied. 'My dearest, today I am not feeling well at all. I will definitely come tomorrow. I cannot endure being apart from you. Please forgive me for my absence today ... Your ever loving ...' etc.

At last, I fell asleep. I must have slept for about half an hour when the same person for whom I was recently his ever loving etc. being restless for my company had come knocking at my door. Poor man, he is elderly, his hair is fairly white. He also has a beard though it is not a long one. He often suffers from back pains, and is a semi-invalid. The vision in one of his eyes is very poor; last winter the right side of his body was affected by paralysis, but what can he do? Despite all his infirmities he is mad about me. He is well heeled and that is why I also pay him attention. On receiving my reply that I was (heaven-forbid) unwell, he got so alarmed that he had rushed here himself.

When he comes here in such a state, he sits outside for a few minutes to collect his breath before he enters. I watch this performance out of the corner of my eye. Weeping once during each meeting is the usual expression of his love for me. Putting his arm around my neck he begins, 'My dearest' (with the emphasis sometimes on 'my' sometimes on 'dearest') ... in the middle ofhis speech, he breaks down completely and tears fall from his eyes into the thick growth of his beard, until that beard transmits those drops to my cheeks and when this tax has been paid by him, he repeats for the thousandth the time his proclamation of love. Again he goes into all the details and from time to time expects me to shower praises. 'Look at my age and these sacrifices for your love dearest ... by God had it been someone else he would have died ...' The word 'dearest' becomes like the metre of a poem from his frequent use. He never leaves before spending at least three or four hours, and by the time he gets to the door he has recited two or three verses of Daagh. Oh I forgot to tell you when I am with him, there is never a third person, we are completely alone ... so he sings, and oh how he sings! So this is how the evening passed. Then it was time for me to set up shop again.

Now you know that this is the same Laila who sometimes whilst in your embrace tells you her philosophy of life. This is the woman whose wounds are hidden from your limited gaze. Every day and every evening she sells the most precious commodity of her existence. You call such a woman armed, you do not see the pain and anguish in her smile which has shaken the foundations of her life. Can you not see the picture of death beneath the corpse, which lies covered in silk and velvet? Do you think that this beautiful who is woman laughing is *really* laughing? Do you think that she is immune from the serpent's poison and that she has not seen the serpent's coils around her neck? If only you realised that your serpent's poison is not even a pin prick compared to her wounds. But how would you know the ways in which the most precious commodity of life is sold for a fistful of wheat? Come, come and see a few moments in a day of my life. You sometimes cry and think that 'this is love' but I laugh, because laughing is a part of my profession and because I cannot cry. From where can I produce tears? My laughter is my stock-in-trade. Listen to my words and remember them! Say whatever you want to a ruined woman, but do not taunt her. You simply have no idea of her misfortunes and what she has to go through.

The ninth letter

How confused life is ... the sins of man, his weakness and oppressions; the tyranny of force over infirmity, that of the strong over the weak, the big fish waiting open-mouthed to swallow the little fish, the massive weight of the elephant's foot which annihilates the ants; the arrogant rider and his undisciplined horse and the blind and the deaf who walk along the road—are these all destined by Providence? Is this the law of Nature? Is this why man was made the lord of creation, so that men should tear each other to pieces and shed rivers of blood over each crust of bread and each grain of wheat? Is the world filled with beasts in human form so that they can banish tranquillity and contentment from every home on God's earth?

But why should you waste your moments contemplating these realities of life? Where do you have the time to do so? You are embroiled in your love for me. When a man loves a woman, he is besotted by her and is prey to a base but strong feeling which says, 'This woman is beautiful and desirable; she is your prey and an offering to your sensuality.' Man has named his sensual longings *love*. He cages his conscience and hides the cage with a black cover, so that his conscience can neither see nor hear anything. He illuminates his sensuality and goes down the path of sin. No other creation of God has this ability to deceive its conscience to the extent that man has, as if man is the lord of creation only by virtue of his deceit and wickedness. Both these qualities are displayed in his treatment of women. On her part, a woman kneels reverently before a man where deceitfulness and treachery are concerned. Without doubt, a man is far superior to a woman in this skill. When a man says, 'I am fond of her', what he really means is that he wishes that particular woman to share his bed. But a man hides this sordid face of his lust behind a veil of words.

A woman is tricked by a man's entrancing and sweet words in the same manner as a bird is lured by the seed scattered on top of the net—too late a woman realises what a man's so-called love really means. By this time, the water is over her head.

It is said that a woman is unfortunate, and the world considers a woman to be by nature deceitful and conniving whilst a man is by nature straightforward and innocent. Oh God! That a man should be regarded as straightforward and a woman as conniving! If only someone would ask my opinion! I am a woman whose life contradicts this claim. When my so-called true and faithful lovers come to me in privacy, at such a time ask me what a variety of antics of their 'straightforwardness' I have to put up with. A man's so-called love is a *ghazal* whose objective and conclusion is my immodest bed. When such men come and sit with me and protest their love in a long drawn-out manner by saying, 'I am mad about you, I am besotted by you, I have never loved anyone as much as I love you. You are my life and the queen of my heart. I cannot live without you,' I start laughing inwardly and observe with a cynical gaze how armed with these expressions of love, this man comes towards me, brings his head towards my lap, and his hand travels towards my back—I then judge that the conclusion of the *ghazal* is near. Then for a few days, his passion is intense until his sensuality finds another direction, the man senses that my stale kisses are tired, and his passion cools by slow degrees and it begins to show. One day he disappears and never comes in my direction again. Sometime later I hear that the tide of his passion has turned in another direction. This is the name of this so-called love and this is the distinguishing feature of most men. Whether they are with their wives, or with women of the street, the foundation of their so-called love is often the same. From the depths of the wine house to the height of the tallest *minar* of the mosque, from the biggest moustache to the longest beard, the reality of men is the same. It is beyond any possibility of change.

Adorn yourself in raiment of any colour
I recognise you by your style.

An admirer often comes to see me. 'Only to hear you sing,' he says. The word 'only' is given great emphasis and when he has an opportunity, he narrates very pleasant stories about the mutual love between his wife and himself. 'My wife is one in a million,' he says. 'I have no peace without her. I can swear to you that till today I have never looked with desire at any woman other than my wife.' I am amazed by this revelation. In spite of his private life being so blessed with happiness, why was he honouring me in this way? Finally one day I could contain myself no longer. Having listened and listened to this story of his, I said, 'Sir, for people as fortunate as yourself, it is simply not fitting that you should visit the places of ill repute which we inhabit. How can we provide any substitute for the blessings which are available for you at home?' Looking somewhat ashamed, he said, 'I am fond of music, and this fondness brings me to see you.' I replied, 'Should you so wish, I can teach your wife to sing. Then you will not be put to the trouble of coming and going from my house.' 'That is just not possible,' he said. 'It is contrary to all the traditions of decency.' I told him that if to teach his wife to sing was against the traditions of decent people, surely for him to visit a professional woman like myself could also not be regarded as enhancing decent traditions. He looked taken aback, laughed sheepishly, and said, 'Oh well, please sing a delicious *ghazal* for me ...'

God protect me! Music, which is the magic of the gods, has also been appropriated by man in the service of his sensuality. So that he may cast lustful glances at the beauty of a woman of the street—a man takes refuge in the name of music. But leave music aside, to pander to his desires, he has no inhibitions about invoking the name of God Himself. If a man wants to hold a really desirable woman in his arms, he says that God has allowed him four wives. As if God has licensed man to indulge in sensuality and take His name whilst doing so! The sensuality of man has not left the name of God and His Prophet untarnished—to say nothing of music and the delight of skill.

Your arrow has not left anything in this world for anyone to hunt.

The true beauty of the universe is but food for man's carnal desires. He does not listen to a woman's song because music creates any harmony in his soul, he feigns a taste for music to get to the woman; he wishes that through music, passion may be aroused. I know these admirers of music very well indeed. May God damn these fraudsters! When they sway to the tune of my music and shake their heads, and prance around, then the reason for their intoxication becomes so clear to me that I have often wanted to bash these men in a public gathering with my *sarangi*. These beasts consider that their sensuality is the beneficiary of the blessings of Nature and they consider it entirely legitimate to abuse these blessings. Nature created the grape, and they have fermented and rotted it to make alcohol, so that it can support them in their sins. Nature created flowers and men plucked them, scattered them, and crushed them on their sin-laden beds. Nature has created iron and men have turned it into swords which they have stained with each other's blood. Everything which God has granted to us to secure our lives and property has been appropriated for force of oppression. Men have caged the delightful and beautiful birds which Nature created to adorn forests and gardens. Although the theme of the songs of these birds is freedom, their wings have been deprived of the power of flight. Women are in the same situation. These rights of ownership, which are announced loudly and called a part of religion, culture, and manners; these examples of superiority and excellence which are being advertised in madrasahs and mosques and in the cells of religious teachers—all these are merely manifestations of lesser, as well as superior forces, of oppression. It is not an announcement or an advertisement. It is a deception. You constantly tell me that I am the most valuable asset of your life. This is only true to the extent that if you had your own way you would cage me like a bird and my beauty would be an asset recorded in the ledger of your sensuality. Shame on you, you hard-hearted trafficker of human beauty!

The tenth letter

If you keep collecting these fragments of mine, and some day have them printed and published, whether or not your name is respected in the educated circles of this country, you will certainly be famous! In the market where Beauty is a commodity, I have become so well known, that now people like you, who by the grace of God are wealthy and educated, seek closer acquaintance with me. By such means, these people can become quite respected leaders. Nowadays all that is needed for leadership is a loud mouth and a trumpet. Anybody who gets 'published' in the newspapers can easily aspire to leadership. If you can get into print, you too can become a guide for the community. This gender-inspired revolution is not at all difficult. A few bottles of printing ink and a few stones—a leader is made up of these elements. If among the revered leaders of India there is anyone who wishes to add an extra string to his bow, I can offer him the right to the authorship of these pages. Or if the occupiers of the *mehrabs* and pulpits of mosques need their stature to be further enhanced and polished, they too can issue orders and fatwas for a jihad against these pages. There is little doubt that by waging a jihad against the shamelessness of a woman of the street their standing will be greatly enhanced. When they pronounce that publishing the intimate feelings of an unchaste prostitute in this country is a crime against decency, they will emphasise their point by prefacing their words with phrases like 'the word of God' and 'the words of the Prophet'. In these circumstances, who will disagree with them? When they stand on the stage, roll up their wide sleeves, and shriek, 'This whore, who is staining the purity of our coming generations, who is casting aspersions on those conceived in lawful wedlock, should be stoned!' then who knows what will become of me? Some religious divine person may make such announcements in Delhi, in Kanpur, in Patna, in Dildarnagar, in Farrukhabad, in Timbaktu (these days there are as many religious parties as there are religious scholars) and if they start stoning my house, then my peace and tranquility will be destroyed. Many well-known and highly respected figures will then find it problematic to visit me, and it will be difficult to maintain peace and tranquility. In short, the publication of these pages will be like a red rag to a great many raging bulls and I will be burnt to a cinder in the flames of their fury. Putting amusement aside, the fact is that I would have bowed my head before every sacred cloak if the wearer of that sacred cloak had not bowed his head into the folds of my sari!

These pages may or may not be published; whether or not a man, driven by sensuality, listens to the voice of a woman whom he has wronged, the voice which has been raised cannot be silenced. Water that constantly falls drop by drop upon a stone will one day make a hole in the stone. Today it is difficult to convince a selfish world which does not comprehend the truth and which worships appearances, but that day too will come when there will be holes in stones. Redoubtable opponents will be forced to bow their heads. Today we have a mark of shame on our forehead—loathe us as much as you like. Exaggerate and advertise our weaknesses as much as you like and obtain a certificate of superiority. Today in public it is beneath the dignity of a respected and arrogant man to acknowledge that we too are Muslims. But it is another matter that this same man under the cover of night, driven by his carnal desires, will keep his head at the feet of a whore until dawn! Have you ever thought what it is that is called 'sin'? Sin is that wrong practice that cannot be hidden and which becomes visible. The sin that remains hidden is not a sin. In your tradition of decency, disgrace is a sin. If the sin is a secret, it's permitted. If leprous spots are hidden beneath your clothes, you are certainly not a leper. Only that which is visible is a fault. The biggest column supporting your structure of decency is concealment. But a man turns a blind eye to these endless double standards in his life and he fills the world's ears with stories of the connivance and wickedness of women. Perhaps you too can smell the stench of connivance in these words of mine.

Woman is conniving. Woman who cannot even take a step towards a man until a man himself takes a step towards her—she is conniving! A woman who cannot even give vent to her feelings until a man swears constantly about the intensity of his love and repeats these stories a hundred times, is conniving. A woman clasps the arm of the worst man possible, endures all the hardships of life and never even mentions the wrongs done to her. She cries without tears, she screams voicelessly, she sees everything, even through closed eyes, but she endures it all and says nothing. Can this be called a woman's connivance? Now consider a man's truthfulness and high sincerity. He comes to a woman. His lips are parched and his hands are cold. He brings with him all the trappings of passion and love, his tale of love is lengthy, he goes on about the pain of separation, and weeps as if his heart would break. He clasps the covering around the woman's head and ties it to the foot of Heaven's throne. He proclaims, 'Oh woman, my spirit calls to your spirit.' He cites his noble nature in support of his emotions and desires. He says to the woman, 'You are weak my love! I am your protector. You are deficient in knowledge I bring you the light of knowledge. You cannot help yourself. I am your helper. You are a sacred trust which God has given to me.' He keeps talking in this vein until ...

... his cold bestiality is warmed by the blood coursing though his veins. His dry lips are moistened by the lips of the woman. The long tale of love finally ends on a solitary note. The pangs of separation are cured by one transient draught of physical union, the covering that was tied to Heavens' throne falls to the ground, the soul of the woman which was being sought disappears like a mirage. Instead of the refrain 'My soul is calling yours ... ' a man's sensuality speaks and says, 'Oh woman, my body desires yours'. Appeals to Nature are cast aside and the ogre of lust decides that even if a thousand women are sacrificed at the altar of man's sensuality it doesn't matter. This sacred trust given by God becomes, in the seclusion of privacy, a captive of man's sensual desires. Thousands of ships are lost in the stormy ocean of man's desire. Like all those other ships, this one ship also sinks. A whirlpool forms on the surface of the water, then the water becomes level once again, as if the ship never sank. A tiger having eaten his fill sleeps with the innocence of a dove. Ask the hind whose entire being and spirit has been torn to pieces by the teeth of this beast, how sharp his blood covered teeth are.

Go, and if you can, try to put a price on these words which spring from the depths of my being. Your youth, which you value so highly—which every man values highly—has been put in its correct perspective by my words ... Go!

The eleventh letter

Have you ever looked at your past life through the mirror of your conscience? Do you even have the capacity to do so? The wanton behaviour of your youth must have cracked that mirror to pieces. If there is any piece which remains, find it and tie it in a knot. When the ardour of youth cools ... then this piece may come in useful.

Yesterday evening, I was alone simply because I wanted to be alone. The outward demonstrations of so-called affection, an aspect of the lust of men, sometimes wears out even a professional performer like myself. Not that there is any shortage of people who wish to share my intimacy. When is there ever a shortage of such admirers? If it isn't one, it's another. The truth is that I feigned a headache and from early evening, had the door of my house locked. Even then Khan Sahib[1] paid me a visit and left after announcing his presence. Mir Sahib coughed and spluttered outside my door for a long time. Sheikh Ji also walked up and down the road outside for a while. Finally he left. Sahu Sahib also sounded the horn of his car beneath my wall for a long time, I regret that he left disappointed. Editor Sahib also mounted a few attacks but could not get to me. Vakil Sahib's man came and left after banging on my door a few times. In this way, all those who are the custodians of my attractions kept calling my name till late at night before going back to their homes. I put my head on my pillow and waited for sleep ... as if this evening was my holiday!

In the evening, I had my bed sheets and pillow cases changed. One day you perceptively remarked that my bed smelt of all kinds of combined passion. Sometimes you hit the nail on the head; you are witty, but you are no philosopher of pity. A lover should definitely be a philosopher. The fact is that being disgusted with

1. Khan Sahib, Mir Sahib, Sheikh Ji, Sahu Sahib, Editor Sahib and Vakil Sahib are the various admirers of Laila

this assortment of passion, I had all my bed clothes changed. Alas, you just don't know how soiled every fibre of this bedding is! Had you known, you would never have stepped into my bed. What paroxysms overcome you at the extravagance of my bed, as if there is a rival under every wrinkle of the sheets. In truth, this is not incorrect. But what can you say to those idiots who are simply dying to rest in this bed? It is as if they are envious of others having egg on their faces—why should they not have egg on their faces too?

My sleep is not my own. Along with my beauty, I also sell my sleep. The demands of men make no allowance for the demands of Nature. When a man buys a woman for the night, all her faculties, mental and physical, become that man's property. If she laughs, her laughter is not her own, if she cries, it is the same. Her dreams are not hers, her bed is not hers—man is the god of everything. That womanliness, that femininity, in the blooming of which Nature has expended her utmost poetic skill and her extreme talents, of which I certainly was given my share at birth—all of it—I no longer have. I also had my share of youthful zest from Nature, I also brought my collective potentialities into the world, but now where are they? Now my existence is confined to outward appearance, it is a golden container in which there was once a certificate of life. That certificate has now been lost. But around the container there is a crowd of people who are admirers of the outward form. The paper is certainly beautiful, but there is no inner light. Let me tell you what happened to me in the evening.

Last night there was nobody with me in my private quarters, but there was a candle burning on the floor. Absorbed in my thoughts, I looked at the candle. As soon as my eyes fell on the candle, I was riveted. I was in a trance, neither asleep nor awake. My eyes were drowsy with sleep but my mind was still alert. The darkness of the room was a black sheet with a deep chasm. A succession of pictures which were familiar to me flickered past this casement window.... This is my teacher's room. I am standing at the door with a doll in my hands. A lovely woman is calling to me, she is my mother. A handsome distinguished tall man is coming towards me, that is my father ... this pleasing building is my school. We are going somewhere. This is a railway station ... with my father is a good looking young man, he is the picture of masculine beauty which has not yet reached full maturity—this is my betrothed with whom I should have passed my youth and my old age.... I am looking at him with lowered glances as if I am not looking at him at all. A sensation races through my body—a sign of physical maturity whose intensity is beyond the capacity either of the written or spoken word to convey. A man can never understand this sensation which a woman feels. Even the flame of the candle flickered. Then a graceful, pleasing young man about twenty-two years, passed by this window.... This was the first man in my life who made me a woman, but not a wife, who plucked me like a flower from its stem and for a few days wore me as a garland around his neck, then crushed me and threw me into the dirt. This beastly man brought me, a maiden, to the pass where you see me today; he was the one who made me what I now seem to be! ... A gust of wind blew at the window. The flame flickered and went out! I had fallen asleep. However, the recesses of my mind had transported me to a place where a stranger's thoughts cannot reach, and there these pictures had been stored. My mind preserved a picture which completely depicts my past life. My treasure trove of love is secure and is mine alone; no one can intrude upon it. At night in the flickering flame I again saw the picture of my earlier life. I returned to the life of a pure maiden ... but in the light of day I see serpents coiled around the treasure of my memory. You are also one of those serpents. I cannot reach that treasure. You, and people like you, will not allow me to reach it. The shrill demands of your passion blocks even my thoughts from finding those paths. Your protestations of love do not leave me a moment in which I can indulge in the privacy of my thoughts.

When I awoke in the morning, the candle had burnt out and the rays of the sun shone upon the floor. How fast a candle burns! The quicker it burns, the quicker the flame is extinguished. The flame of my life at the moment is in full blaze and God willing will soon be extinguished. I am throwing away my life with both hands. You, and others like you, should come and raid what capital remains in my disordered life. This capital is an unbearable burden around my neck. Raid it as fast as you can. I will be greatly in your debt!

The twelfth letter

When people want to vomit they drink *sikanjbin* and tickle their throats with a feather. Fortunately, I do not need to resort to this method. I neither drink *sikanjbin* nor use a feather. There is a much easier and more effective method to make me sick, which is reading a few love letters from my admirers. How repellent your elaborate lies are! The exaggerated ornamental style, the hypocritical descriptions of the state of your heart—what draughts of bitterness I have to taste!

My admirers amalgamate their protestations of love in prose with proclamations of undying affection in verse. If I were not a bit of a philosopher, these posturings of love, and this sensual delirium would have driven me insane! When you people construct towers higher than the sun and the moon in praise of my beauty, the foundations of this edifice being only paper, I then cry at your lack of intelligence. You people do not know the distance between beauty and ugliness. When you praise a flower, does the true beauty of the flower dwell inside the flower? You regard the day as being light and the night as being dark. Does this mean that day and night have any specific natural features by which they are distinguished? If your mind was functioning properly, you would try to focus on this small point that good–bad, happy–unhappy, black–white, all these distinctions are not inherent in the elements themselves, but depend upon your mental attitude. In essence, nothing is good or bad, neither black nor white. You have adopted all these labels. What pleases you is good. What offends your ears or your eyes is bad. Everyone judges the character of things according to their own tastes and inclinations. Whether he praises or criticises, the standards which a man establishes in his relations with a woman relates to the gratification of his sensuality and he expects a woman to accept this standard, as if a woman has no right of choice at all in this matter. Her sole purpose is that—

> *...if the king says it is night, one should say,*
> *'There is the moon, there are the Pleiades ...'*

If a man sharpens the points of his moustache and becomes the Kaiser of Germany, then understand that a woman is obliged to praise this pose, or if some nobleman wears an *angarkha*, he is confident that no woman will look at him without being spellbound. Again, if a man's hair is well groomed he is confident that a woman will definitely be smitten by his hair style. I have often observed these points in my throng of narcissistic admirers. If I find a man's voice appealing, he wants me to sing the praises of his hair style. If I like some man's straightforward manner, he, in order to captivate me, will waste his time playing the fool. Or again, if I like a cultured man's style of speech, he will himself hold forth upon his stylish manner of dress. How different and how far removed from each other is the psychology of men and women! A man, like an independent ruler, expects that a woman should like what he likes, and she should consider desirable what in his opinion is desirable. A man considers it a woman's duty to obey because he feels that men are superior, they are the rulers and the law is made by them.

Your letters are lengthy, verbose and meaningless. They are full of the trials and sufferings which your love has undergone and full of innuendoes which in your understanding are delightfully witty but which, as far as I am concerned, are coarse in the extreme. You seem to think that this is the way to possess a woman's heart, although you are unaware that in my heart of hearts I consider these absurd expressions of love to be quite ridiculous! I already have a pile of your letters and I am afraid that if things continue in this manner for much longer, many boxes in my house will be full of this rubbish. In future whenever I succeed in snaring the editor of a newspaper or the owner of a printing press in my spider's web, I shall request them to publish these literary jewels. By then doubtless you will have committed suicide! The undoubted publicity which this tragic event will definitely generate for your name will be entirely appropriate. The whole world will resound with praises of these 'literary' pieces of yours and trumpeters will compose new refrains in their honour. For your sake, I myself will write a foreword to these sayings of yours although such an exercise would in fact be appropriate for *Qais bin Umar*.

The fact is that you are entirely wrong in thinking that I chuck away these priceless expressions of love and affection. According to you, I fling them into the waste basket, but at the very least I do assure you that if there is anyone remaining in my lineage—at present this does not seem likely—then this literary pile of yours will be cherished and kept safe from one generation to the next.

You are wrong in thinking that I do not value these expressions of your regard. Do not be downhearted; do not allow your self-esteem to be slighted. I know that as you read this letter your anger will only increase. But in all truthfulness I can tell you that whatever I have said in reply to your complaint must suffice. I cannot say any more or any less with truth. Some day when you come to see me, I will show you several writings similar to yours and many others which express courtesy and a longing to meet; they contain phrases like 'being united' and expressions such as 'I am one who will give his life for you'. All these recipes of unfulfilled, unsatisfied longing and those doomed to sorrow are either copies of your letters, or pages from letters that you have written. Perhaps you wish that I also would waste lots of time in replying to your proposals? You tell me whether I should concentrate on my activities, earn my living, search for support to enable me to sustain myself, worry about increasing the number of my clients, or whether I should just sit and sing praises of your literary taste and style.

You praise my letters in amazement, as if only men are capable of elegant composition! This in spite of the intensely interesting letters which I write to you! You complain of my lack of feeling. You don't seem to realise that the detailed description of my mental and emotional state, which my letters to you contain, can hardly be said to show a lack of feeling. My book of life is fully sufficient for my admirers. Many have come and many have gone tearfully professing their love. I swear to you that I have not revealed even one page of what I write to you to any of my admirers. I am fond of you ... though only slightly. Suffice it to say that I am fond of you to the extent that I do not wish to deceive you ... but you obstinately insist on pulling a corpse out of the grave. Don't persist in stirring this heap of ashes. Perchance there may be a live ember which for no reason will burn your fingers. Nothing will be gained thereby.

Remember that even though this soiled body may have been bared before thousands of men, my soul will never be bared before anyone. But I do admit that when that person comes along who is entitled and who has the capacity to see my soul bared it will be a different story. If you feel bored, then come to my house around four o'clock on any afternoon and you will see that just as your letters relate and embellish the story of your love, I too attempt to increase my allure for people like you. See how I contrive to produce points at the end of my eyelashes, how the sparkle in the eyes is increased, how the hair is coiffed and arranged, how my cheeks are reddened, how the nails are manicured, how the lines of the eyebrows are made up to be dagger sharp, how red skeins are created in the eyes ... then let the competition between us begin—let there be a contest of our expertise and intellect. Every day, I shall invent something new and every day you will write eulogies to me in a new manner.

The thirteenth letter

Two children of Nature said to one another, 'Come, let's build a boat.' They built a small boat and fastened its planks with loving care and sailed it on the pretty pond in their garden, where the fragrant spring breeze made little waves on the pond on which the little vessel swayed to and fro. That boat was neither made of paper, nor wood, nor iron, but it was even more fragile than paper. The builders of the boat did not realise how very fragile such boats are. They thought that since the boat would only sail in a small pond in a small garden—a pond, which would be unaffected by storms and waves—there was no need to build the boat securely. They forgot that even a boat built to sail on a pond one day has to contend with stormy seas and swollen rivers. A pond can turn into a river or an ocean ... They forgot these dangers, but being oblivious to danger does not lessen it—that is the immutable law of providence!

The rains came. The rain was torrential and as a result the streams and rivers swelled on all sides. Sheets of water covered the flower beds. The trees of the forest could not withstand the force of the water and the gusts of wind. There was no low-lying area which was not under water. All the lakes in the vicinity were flooded with water and burst their banks as if they had joined hands to surround human habitation. Huge fields became islands. The pond on which the little boat sailed became a river and started to flow. The little boat, which could not even withstand a breeze, was trapped in the midst of the flood. The flood waters dragged the little boat towards its doom. Like the ruler of the jungle who drags the unsuspecting deer in his jaws, this flood of doom claimed its prey. As long as it was able to—and how much strength did the little boat have anyway—it tried to keep upright, but there was nothing to help it. The builders of the boat were oblivious of its fate. How hard they had worked to build the boat, and how easily they had forgotten it! The water of the lake and the winds (as if they were conspiring together) pulled the little battered boat hither and thither for a couple of days and then with a final shove, abandoned it.

On one side, in the slime, where frogs croak, there is a pile of rotting logs. Some of the logs were in the sludge, some outside it. In the morning, the farmer going to his fields walks over this stinking rubbish. He is unaware that in among this stinking rubbish there are a few planks of some boat which are lying there rotting. This was a boat which was built with great enthusiasm by its builders.

If only someone could summon those oblivious boat builders! If they are so inclined, there is still enough strength in these planks for a new boat to be built. This boat will not be as strong as the previous one, but it will still be fit to sail on the stream in the little garden. Otherwise, after a little while the planks will rot completely and become rubbish. These careless people have built many many such boats. The boats are put into water. They are broken. They are sunk and thrown into the mud. Is there a fisherman anywhere who can put the planks of this broken boat together again? Who can procure a sail and an anchor for this boat from somewhere?

My gracious lover! The fable I have narrated, is that of my life. When the blood of youth runs hot—a man's blood—at such a time these fables make no sense. Let the heat of this fiery flood, this fire that burns within you, cool a little. Once the fever of sensuality has subsided, then, like a mature man, listen to the story of a woman. At the moment, you are not a man in the truest sense of the word, nor am I truly a woman as far as you are concerned. At present, both of us are simply animals ... male and female. You think that you are my lover. Nothing could be further from the truth. In spite of your beard and moustache, you are an infant who being attracted by the sight of a glowing ember, picks up the ember in his hand. When the ember blisters his hand, he cries out, 'Oh, I am dying ... I am dying for the love of Laila.' Then in a few days, the very same hand stretches out towards things which glow, and the hand touches new embers. Again the hand is blistered, again, it heals—and so it happens, again and again.

The explanation of this confused dream is not easy to find, and it takes a long time to be found. If you can find an explanation, then come and see me. I am an example of a ruined life, and there are few in this world who are prepared to listen. The day I begin to tell you the story of my life, I will tell you that like me there are countless thousands of ill-used women. They do not require the love or mercy of you heartless tyrants, they require justice!

The fourteenth letter

Yesterday you must have seen seated in my house a young man upon whose face a moustache had not yet formed. A few days ago, this poor chap was in the grip of a serious illness—he was under the mistaken impression that I loved him! I tried my level best to disabuse him, but he was convinced that even though I loved him, I could not express my feelings fully because of my womanly shyness. I could not be open and candid. Perhaps he was waiting for the day when I would lose self-control and lay my head at his feet! He mistook my perverseness for secretiveness of affection. Our association dates from the day when you saw me with him in the park. The price of that first evening was very high. I deal in very large amounts. That evening, the poor chap came very carefully into my private parlour. In watching his fastidious manners, I forgot the way I had to behave. The limit was reached when he sat close to me and a lot of time was wasted as he constantly tried to admire his shins, the roundness of his arms and the pleasing proportions of his body. Instead of becoming intimate, he said he was expecting me to make the first move.

For a long time, he put his elbow upon my pillow in a lover-like manner. I started to stretch, he changed his position. I began to yawn and he began to tidy his hair. I got fed up and changed my position and he in turn began to smooth his pajama over his shins. I started to hum a tune and he began to adjust the strap of his golden watch. Eventually, waiting became unbearable and when he showed no signs of, as it were, getting down to business, I became exasperated and decided that I would sort him out. Listen to the conversation I had with him:

I : How are you feeling at present?

He : Thank you, I am well.

I : Why did you remember me?

He : Why does a man remember a woman?

I : You tell me.

He : What can I tell you. You understand.

I : Tell me clearly, what is your purpose?

He : Purpose? My purpose is simply that which every man has with every woman.

I : You mean?

He : How can I explain it to you?

I : Say something at least.

He : Um ... Umm

I : Damn this pointless talk! Why don't you say that you wish to receive value for your money?

He : Fine, I love you and have been crazy about you for a long time.

I : Forget about loving me and being crazy about me ... You've paid money and you now want its value.

He : (Amazed) What are you saying? I want your love.

I : My dear Sir! Love cannot be bought. Nor is love for sale.

He : Then, do you find me repulsive?

I : You may be repulsive, but I do not find your money so.

He : But I love you, become mine.

I : What rubbish is this, young man! You have purchased my body for this evening. My body is at your disposal. This fact is as obvious as the sheet and pillow on this bed which you can purchase from the bazaar, a this electric lamp or coal, which you have purchased to burn in your fireplace for your comfort. Think carefully about what you buy. What have you bought? My body and its pink flesh, my perfumed apparel, the sparkle in my beautiful eyes, my soft fingers, the music in my voice, in short, all my outward beauty. Apart from this you have purchased nothing! You have purchased an envelope, a velvet covering over food, just remember that you have not purchased this woman. Nor can you ever purchase what is inside this body. You have bought only this body and whatever is outside. Come on, let us go to sleep.

This man had been listening silently ... He neither lifted his eyes to meet mine nor did he open his mouth. After being silent for a while, he got up and said: 'Forgive me, I have purchased the wrong article. I want a real woman. I do not require just a body.' I replied, 'What a pity! I too have no choice. But I have no hesitation in offering you what is for sale.' 'Is it not possible,' he said, 'for me to come here from time to time if not as a lover, then as a discerning friend? Such meetings will be more pleasing to me than this evening. Do I have your permission?'

This is how my friendship with Mumtaz began. Our relationship is free from the tumult of love and desire. He comes and lies on my bed for hours. He has heard from me a part of the story of my life. You, to this day, have not been able to hear even a word, and may be you never will be able to ... The trouble is that you are not my friend and chum, you are merely protesting your love.

Mumtaz comes from time to time. He tells me some interesting story about himself. Listening to some ridiculous incident of my life, he laughs for hours. There is now no trace of the foppishness which he displayed that first evening. Neither is there any trace of that affectation nor that fixation with his dress. This is a new adventure for a professional woman like me. It is clean and innocent, and these days, a source of interest for me ... much more so than your love!

The fifteenth letter

Oh you Majnun of the wilderness! Don't be upset by these titles. I have heard of and seen nawabs who do not have a state—you are also a Majnun of the wilderness in the same way as I am Laila without a velvet cover. You are a Majnun of the city, I am a Laila of the streets! Go and seek your desert and your she-camel—then you and I will some day find the same path. At the moment, as far as I am concerned, your perception is at a very childish stage. When I am in your arms, I laugh heartily at what you say. I tease you and sometimes stroke your soft shiny hair with affection. Do you really think that my whole affection and concentration is not with you? Like a small child who sees the needle of the gramophone going round and round but does not know where the sound comes from, you see my needle revolving all the time—you are aware of the warmth of my body but do not perceive the chill in my heart. You are entirely oblivious of the internal machine which drives the external parts. A lump of flesh and its covering skin is placed next to you. Its outward manifestation is very beautiful, and you, considering yourself in love, regard this as a poetic posy of flowers. But you have always been indifferent to the internal torments which afflict me and you always will be. And with such a collection of perceptions you call a woman foolish? Foolish because my femininity is openly on sale? Foolish because I eat and dress well? Or foolish because God has made me beautiful and the wicked world took away my natural innocence and threw me in the dirt? Did I choose this life for myself at which the sober and the pious look down upon me in scorn? Is this occupation, which is with great solemnity declared sinful and which is paid for with great punctiliousness, my choice? Who was responsible for opening this shop in which I sit and trade my physical charms? Who are the customers who visit me? Who is it that keeps me in business? If I had my way I would drag those turbaned characters who adorn mosques and pulpits, outside their private cells and say to them, 'Come, and for a few days stay with this sinner. If you can spare the time from eating free meals and marrying four times then come and brighten the unfortunate home of this helpless woman whose heart is yet cleaner and purer than those worthies on whose hearts all thirty *paras* of the Quran are imprinted, who set standards of morals and conduct, who wish to measure the length of the pajamas and beards of students, who wash the marks of prayer on their foreheads five times a day, who make the roofs and pulpits of mosques resound with "teach us to follow the right path" and other such verses from the Quran, who make the walls of a school shake with thunderous chants of "accursed unbelievers!"' What is the point of this charade? I have called this exercise, self-deception—which is the cardinal sin of human beings and particularly of man, it is also the prime fruit of his deceiving nature. Self-deception is the sin by which the lamps and lights in the arches of mosques and pulpits are blackened, this is the sin which makes the *lotas* in the mosque impure and compared to them even a woman who sells her chastity is more pure. This impure and shameless life of mine, by the grace of God, is still better than the net cast by these pious people. I trade my chastity and I say that I do so. I am a counterfeit coin and everyone knows that I am counterfeit. I do not claim to be pure gold. I do not take shelter behind a *tasbih* and a perfumed beard to pick pockets and deceive people. Nor do I invoke the *Shariat* for degenerate and sensual ends. My sin is merely that I sell my body because I want, somehow or the other, to attain that state, which the predators of this world have deprived me of. Don't be amazed. The list of my lovers includes many respected inhabitants of mosques and pulpits. The difference between these worthies and others is simply this, that for them even sensuality appears in the guise of *Shariat*. I mean that after a few coarse attempts at affection, there is an offer of marriage to which I reply, 'Sir, I prefer open disgrace to selling my chastity in your sacred sanctuary. Such a marriage will not lessen the sin which you and I will commit. What will certainly happen is that you will be consenting to my activities. By the grace of God, you have three wives sitting at home. You are almost sixty years of age. If I have to share the *valima* feast, the dates of the *nikah* and the *batashas* on which the words, "In the name of God, the beneficent, the merciful", are invoked with three other shareholders, how will I manage?' He got angry and wrote, 'O wretched girl your abode is hellfire wherein you shall abide forever.' I also witness these extraordinary happenings.

This animal yet rational being who is called man is capable of different kinds of assault and different types of deceit. 'Men are the protectors and guides of us women of deficient understanding.' What extraordinary protectors and guides! How amazing that silly sheep should have this complaint and this complaint should have a universal echo! May the wolf be the guide of those who complain! In their black shadows, how many women like me are today leading ruined lives! Their days are dark and their nights are darker. And then they are subject to all kinds of taunts. Today I will stand on the rooftop and openly enquire where are those protectors of ours? Where will I find them? Shall I look in the mosque or in the schoolroom?

The sixteenth letter

Take but one ray of sunlight and also a moonbeam; even if you wished to donate your entire life's wealth, you could not purchase either. The warmth and brightness of a woman's heart is either of more worth than these, or it is freely given. I greatly appreciate the gifts and presents which you shower on me! When have I ever refused to accept them? When have I ever looked at them with scorn? The trouble is that you want to purchase a jewel in a grocery shop. If there is anything to be praised, which is also highly priced, it is my body. Apart from my body, there is nothing that I have to sell. The rest is simply in your mind, which is on the wrong track. A man often says to a woman 'Love me' as if love was a garment which one can take off and put on. Then a man also says, 'You are incapable of loving me, you are not attached to me. I will teach you how to love.' One day a man carried away in a flush of affection told me in a melancholy tone, 'Very well, you say you cannot love me, then wait a few days and see the extent of my feelings. You will have to treasure my love.' What a thought! I told him, 'My good Sir, here I am. Convert your love into practice. I value your tremendous gesture. It may well be that slowly I shall begin to love you.' He was delighted, and I was in his company for a whole year. He asked me countless times, 'Tell me, have you started to love me a little?' Finally, I told him candidly, 'My dear Sir, my love for you is growing stronger every day. But there is a huge problem which I can see. Farewell to our love!' He was disturbed by my remark, 'Tell me what is the matter? Is there someone else?' I pursed my lips and replied, 'My dear Sir, there are more than half a dozen others, but I have developed an attachment to you.' 'Then for heaven's sake tell me what the problem is ...' he asked as if he could remove it in an instant. I replied, 'The problem is that the intensity of my love is growing stronger every day and your pocket is getting steadily emptier. If the one increases and the other lessens, then how is this heavy burden of love to be carried over the uneven rocky path of poverty?' At first he was disturbed. Then he began to understand. He was a self-respecting man. Thereafter, he left and never returned.

You say to me that there is no compassion or justice in my heart. My dear friend! Where is the heart in which these qualities reside? Compassion and justice are not commodities for sale in this market. Look at yourself. You know that my feelings for you are not those which should naturally exist between a man and a woman. Even then you brazenly assault my womanhood and are complacent about your wealth. If tomorrow you were to come across a woman more beautiful than myself, you would make her your conquest, and the day after that, if there was another more beautiful woman, you would behave in the same way. You know very well that I have many admirers like you who have wives at home. Even in their thoughts, those wives are not permitted to stray beyond the four walls of their house. These admirers have small children, who are rightfully entitled to their father's love. They are Nature's trust, a trust which has been bestowed on a human couple in order to carry on the business of life. Their wives are those, even in whose thoughts, no other man can enter. Do they not know why their husband is late in coming home and where he stays half the night? Why is this husband's place in the home empty from morning till night? I have often asked men why they persist in calling me hard-hearted. This is a taunt which does not become them. One wolf seeing another wolf's bloodstained claws and teeth is not entitled to raise objections. If my heart is devoid of justice and mercy, what pray is in your heart?

Repent or tell me, why people usually do not repent of their
own accord?

When I say such things to my so-called lovers, they laugh in a shamefaced way and change the subject. If they are feeling more candid they say, 'What can I do? Your love has enslaved me. Don't think that I do not care about my family, but what can I do about my heart?' Some heart! Their heart is compelled to fall in love with me, my heart finds no contentment even with several lovers. My heart tells me that I cannot have too many admirers. The men are compelled by their feelings for me to cast aside their whole family, but even kicking out these admirers gives me no pleasure! What kind of logic is this? When you get married, and contribute towards increasing the human race remember these words of mine and if even then you are not satisfied with one wife, be good enough to afford her the same freedom of choice that you have had.

I have never understood these double standards applied by men. Whatever moral lapses a man may commit, they do not give rise to half as much censure as even a slip in good manners by a woman can cause. Why does this selfish animal set different standards of decency for himself and for women? In his defence he maintains that religion itself has allowed him four wives at any one time whilst a woman is only allowed one husband. I simply don't believe, whatever your maulvis and priests may choose to say, that Islam has sanctioned the marital arrangements that are at present being practised. I say openly that the plurality of wives is but an excuse for sensuality and lust carried on under the cover of the *Shariat*. It is said that the sensual urges of men require more than one woman for satisfaction. Whereas when a woman is a mother or is expecting a baby, she is incapable of fulfilling a man's sensual appetites for a considerable period of time. I am a woman and I am telling you plainly that one woman is more than enough for a man. That men and women should be obsessed with pursuing their sensual urges is a gross violation of natural instincts. Such behaviour is the result, not of the force of lust, but of mental disturbance, the result of which is that a man, to satisfy his sensuality, is in constant need of a woman. True and natural sensual desire certainly does not require the continuance of such behaviour. Forgive me. Even though I trade my decency, I am after all a woman and cannot express my views on these matters more openly. So far as a woman's sensual desires are concerned, this is a secret which she regards as more valuable than her life. Whatever I have written to you today is more than sufficient. Just remember that one woman is more than enough for one man. The man who in order to pursue his uncontrolled lust and to maintain a number of wives argues that one woman is not enough for one man is a liar and a scoundrel.

If you could refrain from taunting me for self-praise and conceit, I will tell you that even in my present condition as a woman of the street. I am better than those, the beads of whose *tasbih* have been stained by the blackness of their hearts. I am simply the victim of man's lust and of my financial needs. For my needs, I am not lustful and if sometimes such a moment occurs, I have neither the ability to write nor to tell you verbally what I go through at such a time. I look around, and in the inner recesses of my heart there is another woman who is not a part of this perishable body, who asks me, 'When will my man come?' You are unaware that for every woman there is only one man. When a woman finds that one man in this world, then she realises that Heaven is merely another name for this world. Don't be deceived into thinking that every man can become the beloved of every woman. Until now this fact has remained a mystery of Nature. I often think that God has Himself sorted out humanity into couples and sent them into the world. Then men in their foolishness upset this arrangement, and make this whole world a place of woe and then like fools bewail their fate. Destiny? It is simply an incomprehensible term!

When an attempt is made to make a square a circle or to change a circle into a square, or when camels are found in the ocean or fishes in the desert, when the elements of the universe are hidden from sight and the intellect is incapable of contemplation, when wrongs are committed and the consequences of those wrongs not taken into account, when the rules of life are disregarded and the wrong path is chosen, when the true destination is claimed to have been reached and when those are mere claims without any proof—

men cry, 'Alas! *Qismat*!' If *Qismat* has any reality, then accept the fact that the Almighty's rule is tyrannical. Man is helpless and handicapped. If so, then neither sin nor virtue exists. There is no reward for virtuous actions nor is there punishment for sin. I have led a sinful life. That is my destiny. You have ruined your wealth pursuing sensual pleasure. That is your destiny! You tell me that you have qualified in philosophy and psychology. I am merely a helpless woman of deficient understanding. If your learning and superiority can at any time loosen any part of the tangled relationships of life, please let me know!

The seventeenth letter

Why in heaven's name, do people keep bringing God and religion into everything? You are so playful, as to play even with the beard of your father. What has religion got to do with the dark doings in which you and I indulge? Why should God be concerned in our affairs?

You are no learned divine that your love should come dressed in the garment of religion, *fiqh* and the Hadith! I have only a fleeting acquaintance with what you call religion. My knowledge of religion and God springs from second and third grade maulvis who have from time to time got entangled with me and whose faultless diction and recitation I have heard being intoned at appropriate times. But the coarse love professed by such maulvis often comes together with a proposal of marriage. These poor chaps only seem to know one sort of sensuality—the sensuality which in one form or another comes wrapped up in religious terminology. Never mind! I somehow or other manage to escape from their religious strictures and exclamations of damnation but I simply cannot accept the way you are involving the name of God with your professions of love. Leave the work of the world to the world. Don't go further. Neither you nor I know what lies ahead. The basis of your religion and mine is only that it was the religion of our parents. What do you and I know of religion? You by the grace of God are educated, but only like a structure on four pillars laden with books. I, poor wretch, was also once the daughter of a decent respected family. At some point I too had done some religious reading. After this my parents (the flame of their memory still burns like a bright light in some recess of my mind) with great enthusiasm had me educated in Arabic, Persian and Urdu. I finished a few elementary books of education such as *Ma Muqeema*, *Khaliqbari* and *Rahe Nijaat* and read hundreds of Persian and Urdu books. If reading books, saying one's prayers, fasting, and learning the rituals of Hajj make one a Muslim, then I too, am a Muslim. Those who call themselves the purveyors of the Islamic religion do not know any more than this. Had I not been forced into this life of sin, today I too would have been considered more educated than many of those who eat free meals and dates distributed at the time of marriage, and also the special rice at *valimah* dinners. But all the education I had, now serves to embellish the indecent trade in which I am engaged. Just as well-known turbaned men often prostitute their education and excellence for wicked ends, in the same way I also make my education a means of succeeding in my profession. Had I not been born a woman, I would not have been involved in this business of trading in indecency. So far as wickedness and deceit are concerned, I too would have been a religious divine addressed as 'Learned Sir' or 'Respected Sir'. I would have sat on a prayer mat in some private prayer cell, or stood on the pulpit of a mosque, I would have written fatwas, my declarations would have been published. I would have made speeches and would have got to know the highest of the high! Unfortunately, being a woman, I was deceived by men and I am not worthy even to be looked at by respected divines. My life is devoid of any blessings. I am beyond the limits of this maulvi-dominated mystery which is called religion! Then why on earth should I waste my time in these tangles? And in any case, who can solve these riddles? Where are they? Can you solve them? Can the gown and the turban do so? Can the *tasbih* and the *zunnar* solve the problem? Can the Maulvi Hazrat or the Panditji Maharaj solve matters? A son does not understand his father; a brother cannot connect with a brother. A daughter cannot recognise her mother. No one human being can understand another. Despite all the intellectual training the most basic truths are not understood. You are highly educated, wise, and the epitome of culture and manners, despite all this you have not been able to understand me—a lowly, wretched woman. Then why go further? Wade into the river only as far as the ground remains beneath your feet.

All these people who bleat about religion are in fact indulging in a kind of idolatry. Their idol is not made of stone, gold, or silver. Their deity is compounded of their thoughts and their prejudices; personal desire is their god. Instead of the temple their god lives in the Somnath of their mind. It is these gods rather than God Almighty whom these people follow. I ask you whether all the religious education which is imparted to us has enabled us to widen our perceptions and heighten our sensitivity in the slightest degree. Has our knowledge increased? Countless centuries and ages have passed and not even a corner of this mysterious veil which lies over the existence of the universe has been lifted. Religious worthies on the one hand are as clueless as are scholars of science on the other. They parrot a few self-serving maxims! The 'god of religion' which various races have developed is a very frightening element. I despair of it. How much conflict in the world has been spread by the followers of this god! There is no limit either to the blood that has been spilt. All the rules and regulations which are framed for existence are just empty air. Today, a cathedral is built, tomorrow it is broken down. The way of the world and of our own life is just this—destroy and build, build and pull down, try to solve one tangle by creating several more. The philosopher and his philosophy, the physician and his medicine, the logician and his logic, the saint and his saintliness, the mystic and his mysticism—all these are broken vessels, which on the shore of the boundless ocean of life sometimes sink and sometimes bounce on the water. You and I too are broken pieces of millions of sunken vessels which drift along in the tide. This is the reality of our universe! Then in the midst of all this instability there is love, and its profession, claims of affection, complaints of separation, a longing for union, the taunts of rivals, the indifference of lovers and there is Majnun's Laila and Laila's many Majnuns among whom you are one!

The eighteenth letter

You are a lover whose love is unrequited!

Yesterday when your letter arrived, I had just woken up and was preparing myself for business. In front of me was the looking glass. I was shaking the perfume holder and was unwrapping the sari which your rival Rusia Seth[2] had presented to me only yesterday. I wanted to wear this sari so that I could make Sethji feel truly valued and welcome. 'Do put it on,' he had said. I was thinking that if some fool of an admirer were to turn up I would hire a car and drive a few times around the public gardens. When one is wearing a new sari it is essential to go and take the air, otherwise the whole point of a new sari is lost. If women such as myself were to hide their light under a bushel, how would our profession prosper? Just

2. One of Laila's admirers

as advertisements for the theatre and the cinema are distributed on rented vehicles, or just as a famous Punjabi practitioner of allopathy, Unani or Ayurveda has his name written on his car and goes from one big city to another, our attractions too have to be advertised. In order to do so, it is essential to cruise in the public gardens in a motor car. If one did not change one's sari every day, there would be the danger of one's customers getting fed up of looking at the same stale advertisement.

I was lost in my thoughts, when your letter brought the disturbing news that you, God forbid, are bent on committing suicide. And worse still was the news that you intended to do so this very evening. Having read your letter, I was not moved to laughter; instead compassion combined with doubt brought a smile to my lips. I looked at my smile in the mirror for some time. If my lover weeps because his love is unrequited, then I smile in a certain way, if he laughs, then I wear another smile. I have a smile for every occasion—when he threatens to take his life, or when during a moment of intimacy he becomes too informal and I wish to encourage him, or when he asks questions about our union, or when he narrates details of his anguish at our separation, and so on. The armoury of my attractions is equipped with a particular smile for every occasion, just as hunters have specially numbered bullets for snipe, for quail, for deer and then yet another separate number for shooting tigers. When I learnt of your provocative plan, the smile on my lips was that of the custodian of a lunatic asylum, who during the course of his duties, repeatedly witnesses this idiocy on the part of the lunatic inmates.

I have no fear that you would actually carry out your intention, but I am sorry that this evening I will not be able to provide any support. Neither will I be able to go and take care of you, nor will I be able to attend your funeral, because I am going to wear Sethji's sari and I have to show my appreciation by allowing him to lay his head upon my lap. This decision of yours has not surprised me at all because I know only too well that on several occasions you have expressed a wish to leave this unstable world, and on many occasions it is the hope of consummating our relationship that has made you postpone this decision! An expert on diseases is well aware of the symptoms of each disease otherwise he cannot be an expert on the subject. The expert knows that a patient has to suffer through many stages of the disease—a cold, headache, chest pain and pneumonia. He also knows what the condition of that patient will be before he dies. In a similar manner, I too am well aware of how many stages my highly placed admirers have to pass through after the initial exchange of glances, until they reach the point of threatening suicide. Then why does this fever rise and fall? That which you call cholera—if you ask me—is simply indigestion caused by an upset stomach. In such a case how can I believe that you will die or that your death is likely? When the actual ailment is so trivial why should I be anxious? God has given you wealth but no brains! The Almighty has with His blessings balanced out every deprivation. Where He has not bestowed brains, He has bestowed integrity. Where there is great physical strength, it is balanced by weak eyesight. Every individual is equal on the scale. It is just the priority which differs. You have wealth, but lack intelligence and integrity. I am devoid of chastity and feminine prejudice, but I possess intelligence and honesty. Both of us have the same value. My intellect is entitled to ridicule the stupid ways in which you use your wealth; your wealth is entitled to laugh at the way I trade my decency and also at my degradation. What occasion is there for you and me to feel hurt and angry? If you can cultivate this attitude, many of your difficulties will lessen. Then the storms that arise out of our relationship will subside and any possibility of suicide will be ruled out. Be content with what has fallen in your share, and whatever God has granted to me I will patiently accept.

You tell me I am a mere woman and what a web of words I weave! In reply let me tell you that it is men who have taught women this art. Your foolishness has sharpened my brain and your deceit has made me cunning. The deer did not know how to run swiftly in the forest until the tiger attacked it. When man's bestiality assaulted the femininity of woman, then those delicate birds learnt to hide in the thick bushes and deceive the eagle. You employ every kind of deceit and we try every trick we know, to fool you. This is a fair bargain. Why are you annoyed? As you sow, so you reap, and in this world of retaliation this is how things should be arranged.

The nineteenth letter

Many many thanks! On your part, a proposal of marriage and on my part, the sincerest gratitude for the honour you have bestowed on me. Both these sentiments are ridiculous. Are you not aware that my marriage has already taken place? There is only one marriage in a woman's life, and even if a woman unashamedly offers her favours to men a thousand times the situation remains the same. A man's concept of marriage is mainly physical and material. When you men hear the marriage sermon being preached, you imagine a girl or a woman with a beautiful body; you think of her youth and its delights, and then of your wedding night when the delights and delicious youthfulness of a virgin girl will adorn your bed. But when a woman's deepest feelings are touched and she waits for a man, then for such a woman, the man shares a place with God. Such a man is the beginning and the end of a woman's existence. There was no one before him and there will be no one after him. When a man comes to a woman on the first night, he has perhaps satisfied his lust with countless women, but when a woman comes into her husband's arms, on that night she enters a new world, she steps on uncharted ground, and has no idea of what it holds for her.

When a man wants to slake his lust on a constant basis, he offers a woman marriage, but when a woman with bowed head and closed eyes accepts a man with a nod of her head, she, poor unfortunate creature, has no idea what species a man is. What a beast! Even if she loves her husband-to-be, she still does not know how sharp are the teeth of the wolf that hides in sheep's clothing. The woman is only aware of the man's love—she does not know the beast hidden within a man's skin and she will not know for quite some time, not until the bitter experiences of life expose her to what man really is. Woman has been totally surrounded and made helpless by the representatives of society and religion who are only men, and she soon realises that marriage has become her final defeat and man's decisive victory. In the name of God and that of His Holy Prophet (peace be upon Him) a woman becomes a man's property.

Your wealth must have become tired of being showered upon me but you still have no right of ownership over me—a right which you thought your wealth would obtain for you. To heal the bitterness of your defeat, you now take the name of God and His Holy Prophet (peace be upon Him) and want me to sign a bond of enslavement so that I can adorn a niche in your private chamber ... at least until such time as you need me to satisfy your sensual needs. This is the explanation of your proposal! As cunning as a fox, as predatory as a cat, as bloodthirsty as a tiger, a man sends a proposal and invites a woman to join him in a holy marriage blessed by the *Shariat*.

As it happens, one of your brothers, some man or other, undergoes a certain kind of marriage with me every night.

But before this succession of one-night stands began... when I was human, many years ago ... I had already fallen in love. That marriage, unlike other marriages which are normally performed by a Maulana Sahib or a Qazi Sahib, was performed without the assistance of any third party. There was no sermon, no dates were distributed, there was no lawyer, no witness, no wedding guests, there was no question of *meher*, no argument about dowry. There was nothing except a loving glance; that was my marriage, there was offer and acceptance, and there was the seal of love on this solemn assurance. As far as I was concerned, there was true and pure love and as far as he was concerned—that deceiving, faithless, lustful rascal—there was the false and faithless charade of love. I think I have at some point already told you that he was the first man in my life and that this relationship was my first and last love. After a few days, he tired of me, and threw me on to the streets. But I, unfortunate being that I am, despite sharing my bed every evening with some philandering male, even now consider myself a married woman.

Do you have any idea what the state of a woman is who is in love? I swear in God's name that she has no idea what will become of her or what she will do. In her distress and helplessness she looks towards a man and waits for his response. She becomes whatever a man wants her to be. In her imagination she paints all kinds of portraits of the man and she worships those images. Then, when the colours of that portrait are washed off by the floods of her tears, when the man is revealed in his true colours for her to see—she is amazed, shattered and confounded. She says to herself, 'Is this the man I was crazy about?'

I was swept along by the tide of my first love. In a short while, I went too far. From maidenhood's shelter, I came out into the bazaar, and today I stand naked before the world. My advertisement is around my neck, it is emblazoned on my forehead. The world mocks me, turns up its nose, spits in my face and humiliates me in every possible way and then seeks to purchase my favours. All day I am stoned by the world and at night that same world lays its head at my feet!

The scoundrel who tempted me on my first night is today sitting on the chair of justice and is deciding questions of right and wrong. He dispenses justice, he ensures that the scales of justice are equally balanced; he metes out punishment, and he is a supporter of the right of man to have several wives. He lectures women on the need of being obedient to their husbands. He teaches men about their rights of ownership over women. He decides on *meher*, maintenance and divorce, he supports the 'right of *Shariat*', and he is renowned as a proponent of justice.

I want to go to the city and where he lives and seat myself in a strategic spot so that when that embodiment of justice and fair play passes by, I can shout to him and say, 'Listen, you passer-by, you epitome of justice! Just lift up your head and look this way. Even a whore seeks justice! Just look up at me and accept my salutations. And then go on your way having crushed and spurned the love which you once engendered in the heart of this whore! Apply the limitations of *Shariat* to this whore! When this whore was not even a woman but simply an innocent girl, then, O you embodiment of justice, you took advantage of the first flush of her youth.... Do you remember anything at all of that time? Today you accuse me of trading in my indecency, does your penal code regard the flesh trade as such a heinous crime?

You, who sell your intellect, your integrity, and your decency in every sphere of life, be it in trade, in politics, at the altar of learning or upon the judge's chair—is that no sin at all? To weigh the sins of others upon the scales of justice, to sell your mind for a crust of bread in the bazaar, and in return to accept a salary, a monthly stipend, a retainer and other monetary profit is acceptable but what is wrong and deeply sinful is to auction the human body—that body which will shortly become dust. You have, for a few pennies, sold your soul to the Devil. I am accused of trading in indecency because I am openly carrying on my profession and you, by contrast, are a 'Mahatma' simply because you sell your brains, your values, your integrity, and your soul. You can go around selling the gold and the jewellery in your pockets with impunity—no one will ask any questions! But if an empty pocket is sold for a small amount, then that is a serious violation of decency! The manuscripts which are inside an envelope are safe, if you wish you can sell them to the grocer, but if the envelope is torn and tattered, then the seller deserves to lose his head! How people get taken in by appearances! You can strew pomegranate seeds before foolish people in order to draw their money into your pocket, but if the shrivelled skin of a pomegranate is sold, you will hang the seller. Which of us can be said to be trading in indecency—you or I? You trade in your excellent powers of mind and spirit, your court is your high-storeyed building, your office is your slaughterhouse, in colleges, universities, institutions of learning, in government employment, in the columns of newspapers, in the workshops of skills—everywhere your learning and wisdom are being sold at market rates. You increase the worth of your assets by polishing them with gilt just like we apply powder to our cheeks to increase our value. What then is the difference between us? I trade in indecency on a physical basis and you on an intellectual basis.'

When that embodiment of justice, that first man in my life passes below my balcony—oh what will I not tell him! I will shout from the rooftop so that everyone can hear me!

Thoughts such as these come to mind. Then, when an admirer arrives to see me, I start being playful. Tell me truthfully what is the emotional basis of the marriage proposal you sent me? Perhaps you can give me a degree of love, but can you give me the respect and dignity which should belong to a wife? Will the world allow you, once you have made me your wife, to respect me as a wife should be respected? How will you hide the blot on my forehead? If a man says to me, 'For you I will forsake the world,' I will not accept that. When does the world allow any human being to forsake it? The scheming witch clings to everyone. If I enter your home as your wife, instead of you taking me out of my sordid environment and me becoming decent and respectable, my stained past will soil you and people will avoid walking past your house. They will say, 'An impure woman lives in this house. Take care lest her shadow soils us.' Highly self respecting people will tell their wives and daughters, 'The woman in that house is not worth meeting. Don't go in that direction!' I will be isolated from the world like a leper. How long will you be able to endure this embarrassment? As far as our life of pleasure and flirtation is concerned, whether you visit me or I you, even respectable God-fearing people will have no objection. Everyone will say, 'My dear fellow he is still a young man, God has given him wealth; if he is indulging in sexual enjoyment, let him do so. Everyone does so at some stage in their lives.' But once I am in your house as your wife, these very people who made allowances, will pass sentence, turn up their noses and say, 'Goodness Gracious, how badly this boy has turned out. He has blackened the name of his family!' Then how many people will you argue with? To how many people will you explain that you have saved a sinking ship from the flood of life, that you have poured balm on a wound, that instead of doing something wrong, you have waged a struggle for what is right? The whole world will spurn you, and you will contract my leprosy.

In the flush of passion, do not lose sight of the world. God only kills his creation once, but the world kills those who transgress every day in a thousand ways, and even after death, continues to hound them. You can free yourself of your passion for me, but you cannot escape from these worldly gods. Like a pack of hounds, these people will cling to you. Respected figures in the community will proclaim, 'This fellow's conduct is damnable'. Divines will declare, 'This fellow is a fornicator and a transgressor'. Scholars will take your name and utter religious strictures. Other scholars such as 'Mir Sahib' may not say anything, but they will look at you askance. What will you do then? My friend, you must realise that adultery is a gross violation of decency, but only for a woman. Even if a man is an adulterer, he is still considered innocent. Even if a woman is not an adulteress, but maintains any association with strange men, she deserves to be hanged! This law is made by man; no stain on a woman's clothing can ever be washed away, thousands of stains on a man's raiment can be washed clean in one fell swoop. Adultery, alcohol and even worse conduct is not a flaw for a man, it is only a woman who deserves to be hanged for such activities. You can grow the longest beard, wear the largest turban and the longest gown, and sin in the privacy of your room. People will say you are engaged in worship. They will kiss your hands. But every woman who violates the laws, which you men have made, becomes a fallen woman in your eyes. Where can you and I go to escape the octopus-like reach of the all-powerful *Shariat*? The sensible and better course is for you to remain content with our existing association despite it being based on fornication and transgression! Every evening you can marry me and every morning, divorce me and go home ... a marriage which lasts the whole evening, and a divorce which lasts the whole day.

The twentieth letter

I still remember the proposal of marriage which you sent me day before yesterday. I am only too well aware of what love means to you men—you are not so much humans as beasts. Before marriage the love which you have for us women is that which the spider has for the fly. 'Oh my love, be good enough to step into my humble abode. Oh my valued guest, I cannot wait for you to come,'—so the spider speaks and lures the fly. What happens next is well known. But all this happens before marriage. The feeling which a man has for a woman after marriage is that which a master has for the parrots and mynahs in his cage, the household cat, and his pet dog! If the master is in a happy mood, then delicious fruit is fed to the parrot, a full bowl of milk to the cat, and tasty morsels from the table to the dog. But if his lordship is angry or in a bad mood, then he kicks the cage away, the cat is beaten, and the dog whipped. We women are the velvet-skinned cats who walk around the house purring. When we see that the master is happy, we sit in his lap but if the master's look changes, we dare not even appear in his presence. Instead we cower in some corner of the kitchen or in some dark recess. We are always terrified of being pushed away. In fact within the four walls of the house the status of wives and children is that of slave girls. It is the lord and master who allows them a place at his table, who allows them to sleep on his bed. He presents them with fine clothes and adorns them with jewellery. All these gestures spring from the graciousness of the lord and master. The duty of the wives is to accept these offerings with profuse thanks and always remain like suppliants with folded hands because it is thanks to the life of the lord and master that their status and security is preserved.

This is the reality of a woman's existence in a man's house. We are merely there to decorate the niches of your house. We are merely tasty appetisers to whet the appetite of your lust and are put on your table for that purpose. You seek out beautiful women to adorn your house and your bed, you provide us with beautiful clothes and jewellery so that you can create a visual paradise at home for yourselves. You desire our bodies to reek of perfume so that its fragrance is embedded in your bed. You want your lust to be charged by our adornment and decoration. Everything that you shower us with is given in order to satisfy your sensual needs and not because we deserve it but we are still expected to be beholden to you!

When a man searches for a woman to adorn his bed, his chief concern is that she should be beautiful. Regardless of how unattractive and repulsive he himself may be, he wants an attractive woman. Before getting married he sees the girl's face and wants to be reassured. But he never thinks—'What harm is there if a woman wants to see a man's face before marriage?' Are we reduced to being sheep and goats so that you buy us to cut our throats but before you do so you want to feel our hide to make sure we are not too thin? You fight over *meher*, you want a heavy dowry, and in this way you want to purchase what you desire.

One day I went to have a look at a brothel in Bombay. There I saw that needy men come, and ten or twenty practically naked women are paraded before them and offered to them. The men cast shameless and lustful glances at them, they examine them, and then select whom they desire and settle the price. This is a summary of the conversation which takes place over these sacrificial lambs:

> 'Her eyes are good, but her face is too thin.'
> 'Her colouring is not bad, but her body is unattractive.'
> 'She is otherwise not bad, but her eyes are somewhat small.'
> 'Her lips are thick and her nose is small.'
> 'Her teeth are crooked, and her back is fat.'

I ask you—why that day will not come when we too can line up men before us in this way and examine them? Instead of women, men should inhabit brothels, and women should go and fix a price for them. Men should stand in line with folded hands before us and, as men do with us, we should cast heartless and shameless glances at them. We should then summarise their features as follows:

'He is black!'
'He is unattractive.'
'He is one-eyed.'
'He has a squint, and his ears are too big.'
'His beard is unkempt.'
'He is bald.'
'His breath stinks and his teeth are dirty.'

When this happens, then we will wreak dreadful vengeance on you unscrupulous traffickers! Our vengeance will be so terrible, that even the angels will shudder at your plight. Ages will pass and you will be bound in the chains of slavery and bow before women whom today you trample upon mercilessly. Today we are those slaves who carry stones in the desert so that your tower of victory can be built. Your whips lash our shoulders so that we cannot refuse to bear the burden of your sins! No, not even a breath of refusal can we take. We are thrown into rivers so that crocodiles like you can be fed. We are placed before the altars of gods so that the faces of the gods are reddened with our blood. After your victory over us when we are brought on to the battle field wounded and exhausted, your swift horses gallop by and trample us. Will that day never come when women will gouge out your lustful eyes and blind you so that your shameless eyes can never again behold their beauty! They will pour boiling oil in your ears so that you become deaf and can never again delight in the music of a woman. Your bodies will be burnt by fire and bleached in the sun so that there will be no marrow left in your bones!

The twenty-first letter

Yesterday in the process of replying to your proposal of marriage, I became angry. I should not have done so! There is simply no point in being angry with you fools, the best way to sort you lot out is to ridicule and humiliate you. You people do not occupy such a pinnacle of good manners and decency that I should hurt my sensibilities by a display of anger or distress at anything you say. I tried to explain to you yesterday that for unfortunate beings such as myself all routes of escaping from your society are closed. Even if you were to make a woman like me your wife, people would still regard this marriage as little more than a mere result of physical passion. After this if we have children, what will happen to them? A man's attitude to children is just a joke. He does not deny the natural urge to produce children, or the importance of the basic principle. He does not appreciate that the greatest debt of Nature to him is the responsibility to produce healthy, balanced and good natured children so that thereby the human race can continue. Usually, the birth of a child is a misfortune in a man's life. Children are also regarded as unwanted and unwelcome consequences of his sensuality and lust! The birth of children only heightens a man's self-conceit. He considers children an indisputable proof of his masculinity and presents them as such to the world. As a farmer feels that his green fields are a proof of his toil and dedication, so does a man take foolish pride in this demonstration of his dedication. Just as a shepherd is happy at any increase in his flock, when a man becomes a father, like a ruler, he is pleased that the number of his subjects has increased. There is a feeling of strength and arrogance inside a man which is sharpened by the birth of children. When a man takes his child in his lap he does not realise that a child is the natural result of the union of two different sexes, a man simply considers a child to be an incontrovertible proof of his masculinity. And that is all! As if the poor woman had no share in the man's performance. She is simply the child's nurse and amongst all her other duties to her master, there is also this duty to bring up the children. Whatever obligations the children may have is only to their father. The mother plays a minimal part in this scheme of things, although sometimes she also knows ... that this fruit of his polished manners, sitting in his father's lap, is usually the result of an invigorating aphrodisiac which is the product of chemical formulae developed by the sellers of medicine. She is aware to what extent the master's reproductive powers are indebted to the sellers of aphrodisiacs. When man's natural vigour is exhausted by loose living in youth then I have to put up with what is left. I have had so much to do with the sensuality of men, of which day and night I see displays—some of which are ridiculously funny while some are bizarre and shameful. I have often taken packets of aphrodisiacs and other invigorating substances from the pockets of my admirers. When they pop pills in their mouths in the hope that I am not looking, I turn away my gaze. I see everything, but say nothing, when things get too much, I smile, when these people who openly prey on our attractions come to see us and exhaust the sexual powers nature has given them, they then take some decent girl into their lives and take advantage of her youth. No one knows better than I that man's pride in his sexuality is ninety per cent hypocrisy and exaggeration. The bond between men and women which Nature has provided simply for procreation has been virtually extinguished by the hypocrisy of modern morality. There is instead a superficial desire to stimulate unnatural lust which has poisoned men's minds. That true natural bond between man and woman, on which a lasting union is based, has been sacrificed to your lustful desires. Your sexual indulgence in the flush of youth has exhausted all your natural powers, and you now intend to get married. In order to take this step, you will have to be helped by science and by *tibb*. The result will be that you will produce a few lame, one-eyed, malformed, weeping and ailing children. What else can you do? This is the reality of you men, and despite this there is your deceit and arrogance at the prospect of being husbands and fathers!

If you can ever spare a few minutes from protesting your burning love for me, just try to understand that I am telling you about the state of the world in which a woman has to live. It is a world of innuendoes, sighs, tears, and deep wounds. How many different ways I have of telling you but you men are insensitive to deeper truths! You are so blind! Do you not know how your artificially stimulated sexual desires have ruined womens' lives and how they will harm the future of your unborn generations?

The biggest reason behind the ruin of women's health is your tyrannical lust. You consider yourself to be independent kings and you require women to be slaves of your lust. You want a few moments of sexual pleasure and for that you require the compliance of women and no matter what state they are in—whether ill, or handicapped—they should obey the dictates of your lust. If a woman is close to death as a result of bearing your sickly children in rapid succession you are not too bothered. There are many women whom you can marry, and many parents who, under the cover of legal convention, are willing to sell their daughters to you. In this way your lustful activities can continue without interruption. The doe in the forest is born only to be the constant target of the hunter!

The married life of you men is one-sided. Your thirst has blighted innumerable lives. You are only interested in quenching your thirst. Have you ever thought that even a river will eventually run dry? But of course this fact never occurs to you! Whenever you have felt the need, you have taken the name of God and his Prophet (peace be upon Him) to justify your lust. As far as you are concerned, you are doing God a favour by producing lots of weepy, ill-looking, sickly and handicapped children. You justify this to yourself by saying, 'It is the duty of a Muslim to increase the Muslim population.' As if (God forbid), the Almighty had any such expectation from you! Go on producing as many children as you can, no matter whether they are lame or crippled. If your wives die of incessant childbirth so be it, there should be no interruption in this process which will interfere with your lustful acts. No matter if you cannot produce brave fighters for the faith, if you cannot produce free citizens, if you cannot produce hale and hearty children you can instead produce vermin, blind children, diseased children, enslaved children, sweepers and dustmen ... Just go on producing so that the number of the Holy Prophet's (peace be upon Him) followers keeps increasing. Have you ever thought ... my husband-to-be ... how many members of your sex are there who transmit to their wives and children infectious diseases which they have contracted by their immorality and in this manner make their as yet unborn generation fall prey to their sins? These men knowingly get married and produce children and think that there is nothing wrong and this is how things are, there is nothing unusual in the death of wives or in men being afflicted by sexual diseases—why should marriage be affected by these things? When marriage becomes too much of a strain, and a man loses his long-suffering wife, how men shout and cry, 'Oh God, my life is ruined. I am left alone.' This refrain continues for a few days as if the husband is about to follow his wife to the grave but after a few months, talk starts of a second marriage. 'What can I do?' says the man. 'I am greatly inconvenienced. Who will feed me and look after me? I am forced to marry again for the welfare of my children and to lessen my loneliness which I can no longer bear.' Behind these excuses perhaps are hidden the demands of lust which easily propel a man of seventy or eighty years of age into marriage. For a man a second marriage is considered essential but in 'decent' society, widow remarriage is still frowned upon! These are enduring realities. You have perhaps never considered them but I am only too well aware of man's wickedness and deceit.

Sometimes I feel my heart is a huge enclosure in which there are several ferocious growling tigers, sometimes it becomes a deep well from which terrifying sounds ensue. You simply cannot imagine my state. When I contemplate the prospect of spiritual love between us, I see you far away like a tiny star twinkling in the sky. When I contemplate married life with you and its restraints, then I see you as a bloodthirsty wolf with a stinking body and teeth dripping blood! I take my kitten into my lap and stroke it for hours. It sleeps in my lap and for hours I sit on my feet until they go numb. I endure this numbness so that the kitten will not be uncomfortable, which it would be if I moved. Sometimes I see you as a kitten. Perhaps if I married you I would love you as much as I love my kitten ... but ... when I see your face flushed and distorted with sensual desire, I also see your eyes bright with lust, but not with love! When in the grip of your accursed lust, you forget all our conversations of love and seek to subdue my femininity ... I remember your state on such an occasion, my fingers harden and become as firm as a noose. At such a time, I am gripped by a strong urge and I yearn to strangle all my so-called lovers and fill my bedroom with their bodies.

The twenty-second letter

My distracted state over the problem of marriage is worrying you. In your view I have lost my mental equilibrium. You are quite right! I haven't had a minute today. Several of your rivals have been pestering me since morning. After a day or two I'll see how balanced your attitude is. Have you been affected by some mental reform? Have you any idea what equilibrium means? You seem to have forgotten everything that you learnt in the school of love. First take stock of your own equilibrium, then deign to criticise me, a poor stupid woman. You are crazy about my superficial attraction. Is this equilibrium? You make love to me ... this is your idea of equilibrium! You seem to think that equilibrium consists of crying all day for love of me and staying awake all night, day in and day out. When you are awake you spend your time writing love letters to me, when you are asleep you dream about me! If you meet me there is union, otherwise separation. As if this is balanced behaviour! This is the practical routine of your life. The toad which lives in the pond has a similar equilibrium to its life. He jumps about in the slime, and croaks by the edge of the pond. Throughout the rainy season he behaves like this and then disappears for a year until the rains return again. The toad knows all about the goings-on in the pond. Apart from this it knows little else. The equilibrium in your life is just the same as that in the life of the toad. In fact my lovers like you are trapped in the confines of my love as the toad is in the pond. I watch the whole world coming and going around me and people are imprisoned by my physical attraction. I watch people fighting over every dry bone; they are ready to strangle each other for a few paise of profit. To attain personal and political power they are ready to dig each other's graves. There are many people who like you ruin the lives of women and their own youth in satisfying their sensuality. Even when their youth is past, they lay their old age at our feet. There are some who in the guise of spirituality, custom, knowledge and mysticism plunder people's faith and integrity and in the name of God and His Prophet (peace be upon Him) strip people bare. There are many people who have no tranquility in their own lives and give no peace to anyone else either. In such a way, I watch you people fighting, dying, jumping, drowning and ceasing to be. From your bad behaviour I have concluded that the world needs another flood such as the one that took place in the time of Noah which, once and for all, will wipe out life's present system so that no trace is left! Then life's cycle will start again on virgin soil and Nature's equilibrium which you have destroyed, will once again be established in the world. On your inaccurate scale every woman is weighed and if any woman's weight is slight you declare that she is not balanced. For sinners like us, when you establish some institution to restore equilibrium, please include my name in the list of students. At present your equilibrium is so unstable that my slightest smile disturbs it. If my expression grows severe, if a lock of my hair waves in the breeze, if any part of my sari brushes against you, your composure collapses like a wall of sand, and sinks like a paper boat! This, Sir, is your equilibrium. My composure is such that despite tears, sighs and sobs that I endure from morn till night, and the endless love stories told to me by many fools like yourself—I stay firmly in place. My lovers come crying and wailing, and crying and wailing they go, but I remain like a stone wall, like a shady tree in the forest under whose shade all kinds of travellers—hungry, thirsty and weary—find rest for a while, and then go on their way. I stand in the midst of life's vast desert. Storms and lightning encircle me, clouds gather, they bring rain and blow away, winds blow to and fro, the scorching rays of the sun and the cool moonbeam wrap around me and die away. The centre of gravity which I have chosen is fixed and I will remain firmly here all my life. And you presume to teach me equilibrium ... You ... !

The twenty-third letter

I had not quite finished my letter on balance yesterday when an old acquaintance arrived and I got involved in testing his. In this connection, I remembered a list of my lovers which I had started to compile sometime ago. One evening, it was pouring with rain, my lion-hearted lovers were asleep in their own beds; I was sitting alone. In those days an admirer of mine used to propose marriage to me on a daily basis. As I sat, it occurred to me that as there was little that I would leave behind me, I might as well prepare a list of my marriage proposals. After my death, those same fools and scoundrels who today scorn my very existence and pride themselves on being members of the superior sex should at least be made to realise how many distinguished and highly-placed members of this superior sex flouted established conventions of their society and proposed marriage to me. Perhaps this list of mine will give those men's arrogance a shock! To shame you, I am copying out a page of this list. You need not be concerned with actual names. If you can derive pleasure from my brief but subtle hints ... I will consider that you still have an ounce of brain left. Instead of names, I will only write numbers ... your name too will appear somewhere amongst them!

> 'This is Laila's last word—the list of her lovers who proposed marriage to her. This is a legacy of warning to those male rascals who seek to establish the superiority of their sex by defaming women. Laila herself has compiled this list—Laila, daughter of Laila, daughter of Laila—profession: trading in decency, country: India; very intelligent, cunning, shrewd, discerning, mischievous, wicked, sharp-tongued; a wizened old hag of twenty-two years ... Today on this date _____ 1931, at _____ this lot has been written down so that after Laila's death this should be a testimonial to those lovers who wished to marry her.
>
> 1. This predator of women always comes in the morning when my resistance is low in the hope that one day or another he will succeed in one of my weak moments.

2. The lover with the strength of 150 horses! He tramps up my stairs with the heavy tread of a sub-inspector of police bearing a search warrant! My slaps and abuses do not deter him; he keeps pestering me and does not listen to a word I say!
3. In the style of a wild boar, he bows his head and charges. The gust is terrific and I stay out of his way. The force of the gust carries him along; he cannot stop ... This is how I am able to avoid his attacks on every occasion!
4. A crazy bull! He comes head down, tail up, foaming at the mouth. He is very thick skinned ...
5. He has a vast array of alcoholic beverages. I once went with him for a drive, and swore that next time I would not go without wearing armour.
6. His eyes glow like those of a cat, which glow more brightly in the dark. He comes on tiptoe. Inside his soft skin are hidden sharp claws. He sits in a corner with his eyes shut, like a cat waiting for a mouse.
7. All night he plays cards and smokes. In the morning he writes the editorial for the newspaper. In the afternoon he starts making love to me and smokes even more and plays cards with greater zest.
8. The poor chap is ill! He has come to see me straight from the *hakim's matab*. The moment he sees one he has an attack of asthma and goes back.
9. I am a thousand years older than him. He fell in love even before he was born, even before his father was born!
10. Wealthy, coarse, old, he keeps reciting couplets from the *masnavi 'Zahr-e-Ishq'* and Gulzar and Daagh's couplets and keeps weeping as he recites.
11. Richer than No. 10 but not as coarse. He has a wife whose undisputed master he is. He longs for a second marriage. He

already has ten or twelve children; he wants me to produce ten or twelve more.

12. A chatterbox! He is dying, but still survives. He wants to get married but until I reach a decision on this subject, he doesn't want to break off his illicit relations with me. Come what may he wants to stick to me. Like an obstinate fly he is buzzing around me all the time!
13. Very cultured, intelligent, and serious, he has good taste in matters of learning. He studies sexual psychology and keeps explaining to me the essential problems which relate to male–female relations!
14. A leader of the community. In the evening, he addresses gatherings, at night, dressed in homespun, he comes to my house. He keeps trying to enthuse women of the street to be guides of the community, and with his amorous activities he wants to awaken my interest in such matters.
15. He changes colours like a chameleon—sometimes red, sometimes black. All day long he reads *Tilism-e-Hoshruba* and at night comes to talk to me. He smokes a little opium also. A respected maulana! He doesn't come to my house but keeps sending proposals. If he hears that I have a headache, he sends me a *taaweez*. Outwardly, and at the moment, he maintains the demeanour of a father and a revered elderly man. He often expresses anguish at my present circumstances; I have heard that in order that I may be persuaded to marry, he is about to send a *wazifah* or ask me to start ritual prayers.
16. BA, LLB, good looking, well-dressed, shy, he is unable to express his love in words but does so at length in writing! He is not a bad fellow ... a little silly, from being a lover he wants to become a husband. He keeps advancing towards me, I keep retreating, he keeps coming, I become afraid of

> being caught! Behind me is the wall, he is in front, if he keeps coming towards me, how far back can I go? I should run away.'

Have you seen the above and have you understood anything? What a variety of camels pass through the desert that is my life! Despite this I keep each one's halter in my hands and don't let anyone stray! How can I do this without a solid and firm sense of balance? Remember that it is only when you have a firm resolve that your equilibrium will be firm too. Compared to a tyrant, the victims of tyranny develop greater resolve. Oppression itself imparts strength to the oppressed; this is what you call the wickedness and guile of women. This equipment which you have taught us to use is just enough to escape your sharp claws and it is you who have taught us its use!

> *'O morning breeze, thou hast brought all this.'*

The twenty-fourth letter

Your conversation last night reopened my wounds most painfully. I am assessing the present and the future of my life. I do not yet know what conclusion I will arrive at. Please keep away from me for a few days, don't come or write, or send proposals of marriage. After extensive wanderings I have come to a crossroads and I am confused about the direction in which I must go. For God's sake, let me think, recover my composure, and allow me to draw breath!

If, in spite of my request, you come to my house, you will find my door locked. If you write to me I will burn your letter without reading it. Those comes a stage in a person's life when the limits of the present are reached and the boundaries of the future begin. I reached this point last night; my entire spiritual existence is in a state of confusion and perplexity. What has happened? I didn't even know; you crept in like a thief. I kept running like someone who is blind in the hope that this was a means of escape! This is the road to freedom. When I stumbled and opened my eyes, I found myself at the very place from where I wanted to escape. Does destiny consist of such occurrences? Is it destiny when one looks towards the east and reaches west? When instead of soaring into the heavens one finds oneself getting stuck deeper and deeper into the earth? I am a mere plaything of destiny. I want complete solitude for a few days. When I emerge after that, then I shall decide my fate. The river is in spate ... I am tying a knot ... Let me do this ... I have always looked down upon and spurned your amorous advances with ridicule and mockery! Today everything has become too much for me. I beg you to allow me to put an end to it all. Oh God! Oh God! Will even this not be possible?

The twenty-fifth letter

Don't keep writing! I am unable to read, unable to hear, I have no answer. I am being roasted over a fire; the flames are leaping around me. Either this iron will melt and flow away like water or it will become another element in a new mould! Don't bother me. I am burning ... I am dissolving ... I am being annihilated ...

The twenty-sixth letter

You just don't listen, do you? You keep writing, you keep babbling. I am on the threshold of a new world; all the idols of my thoughts are lying about in a state of intoxication. The sacred being whom I have worshipped all my life is deaf to my entreaties. You are opening the doors of a new world for me, a world in which there is death as well as life ... What will I achieve? What will I get? I just do not know!

The twenty-seventh letter

Are you waiting for a reply? What kind of reply? Whose reply? I, too, await a reply! I have asked my destiny a question, and am awaiting a reply. I am gazing at the heavens. Just wait. Don't be so impatient!

The twenty-eighth letter

I have decided! Close the doors of that paradise where you wanted to take me. Such bliss is not for me. My decision is final. Go! Just get out of my life! Go so far away that you can't even find a footprint of mine. Weep as much as you like, bash your head against the wall, die if you want to! Forget completely whatever has passed between us. There was a time when my broken, unfortunate heart was full of light and life. There was only light in my world, the light of love and no such thing as darkness ... no such thing as grief and the darkness of sin. Then a faithless man utterly destroyed the very foundations of this world and went on his way laughing. This is how men proceed to destroy happy homes and move on. They forget! But women remember and sometimes spend their whole lives longing for revenge!

There are three kinds of women, firstly those who unconditionally surrender themselves. A man does not pay much attention to such a woman, who gives her body to him. A man finds such a woman interesting for a short time then forgets her. Then there are those women whose brains are more than equal to that of men, who humble them, and spurn their advances. These are the women a man is crazy about. In the course of my profession, I have learned many secrets of this art, but when it actually comes to humbling an admirer, some corner of my heart feels sorry, this is a weak corner of my heart, and I let the rascal off scot-free. This is my weakness and cowardice, this behaviour in my religion is idolatry and this is the reason why my admirers come in droves to see me. This crowd stays for a night at my caravanserai and moves on. I am happy for things to be so. I am happy that no one remembers me, happy that they all forget. Why don't you also try in any way you can ... in this way in or any other ... to forget me? After the most recent attack on this ruin, which is my heart, I have tried to construct my heart afresh, and this time I have closed every door and window so that no light from the outside world can penetrate the recesses of my heart. But a beam of light from somewhere is penetrating this darkness. Oh God, what a disaster! Is it possible that any corner of my heart has weakened? Perhaps the walls that I have built around myself have developed a crack which is allowing light from outside to come through. Oh God! What will happen if the windows of my heart were to open once more? If there is a living spark in this heap of ashes? Will I once again have to separate all my equipment from my body? Will my sword be unbuckled from my back? Will I again be forced to ask a faithless man to shield me from the vulnerability which falling in love will bring? Will the manifold sins which dwell in my heart be rooted out? Will the bonds of love shackle my body and my innermost being? God Almighty, what is going to happen? I am shivering and shaking; my mind is in a whirl, I am standing before a storm-tossed ocean, and the waves are surging towards me ... Is my boat once again to be beholden to some fisherman so that it may be rescued!

Oh, Lord of the Universe! Let this not be! I will die and be finished. How can a fragile helpless love be superior to the sovereignty of sins? It cannot be. It should not be. Oh God of Love, your arrow will not be able to reach my heart. I am being awakened from a deep sinful sleep. I do not wish to be awakened and would rather that this sleep were the sleep of death. I do not wish to live. I really don't. Why am I then being brought back to life? Has no punishment other than this been determined for my sins?

A voice is repeating these words into my ear, 'You think you can run away. You'll be caught. You wish to sleep the sleep of the dead. You'll be woken up.' In reply I am shouting 'I'll run away, I'll escape. You'll not catch me. I'll die. Don't wake me. Let me dream of death in my sinful sleep. Can it be that the taste of love's poison still lingers on my tongue? Is it this draught of poison that you want me to drink? I absolutely refuse to do so!'

This sinful sleep is the sole solace of my loneliness. I forget my sinfulness and shamelessness and yet I continue to perpetrate such conduct. Hard as flint, cold and insensitive, I neither see nor hear anything. For heaven's sake don't wake me ... Let me sleep. Tread softly in my chamber—if I wake, I shall die!

The largest part of my life is a collection of sighs and tears. Now for a few moments, I want to forget the pain of those sighs and tears and become intoxicated by sinful laughter and forgetfulness. Let me remain in this condition. Don't poison this oblivion and intoxication by the bitter draught of love which becomes poison and infects a woman's heart!

My final decision is that you and I should part forever. I will leave your world far behind me and become untraceable and you, far away from my world, will go back to yours and forget what is past! I was not able to do what I wanted to do, I am a coward and I don't have the guts. Had I been able to do so I would have ended this story by ending my life; I have not even been able to take that step. I am now running away!

The twenty-ninth letter

My heart is in a strange state. You have tried to crack its fortress-like walls. I got ready to sort you out. I tried to defend myself against your assault; I fell, stumbled, picked myself up and sought safety. Why did you have the nerve to try and enter a door which I had locked forever? The star you are gazing at in your love-struck state is about to disappear. You will never again be able to sight it either in heaven or on earth. No, not even if you go on screaming and die from your tears. There is one last weapon which still remains in my armoury. Even though I am an unfortunate woman, I will run away. I am running away in defeat!

By the time you read these lines I will be far away from the world of your love. I will be untraceable and even if you look for me you'll not find me! I can wait no longer. I cannot wait for my harvest to ripen. I shed tears of blood and keep moving I know not where, and as I go, I cast aside all my longings. By the time these seeds grow to ripeness, my life will have ended. I have planted plenty of seeds for generations yet unborn and I have irrigated them with my tears. I will not be there, but my thousands of sisters will be able to reap some benefit from the harvest I have sown. Our love affair is over. Every drop of the tears we shed will be a security for generations yet to come. Remember only this and forget all else. Just forget ... Goodbye!

The thirtieth letter

Moments of dejection and helplessness pass very slowly. If I had not managed to forget the sorrows which beset my heart as a result of the tumult of sin, I too would have found time passing painfully slowly. It has not quite been a year since I escaped and ran away from your impulsive demands. During this period, it is as if centuries of my life have passed by in the same way as for you an evening of union passes! Each day and each month was equal to but a moment in time. After the flood waters receded last year, there was filth, slime, stinking rubbish, and rotting corpses which had not entirely decomposed. I have spent this whole year amongst this dirt.

My final decision to run away was for me like deciding to climb a mountain ... I climbed with great difficulty ... but I managed to climb! You kept pulling me down trying to stop me but I was in such an intensely restless and disturbed state that I pulled away from you and continued running uphill. I did not draw breath until I reached the top! At that point, I was assured by the fact that you were far away, and that you could not catch me! But until I reached the summit of the hill, I did not realise that the descent on the other side would be even more difficult than the climb to the summit. After having exhausted my strength in climbing up, by the time I descended my limbs were out of control and I slithered and slipped all the way down. In spite of all the hindrances you put in my way, I reached the summit but I had no idea what would be in store for me on the other side of the hill. You should know that during the last twelve months, I have thrown my transient existence with even greater vigour than before into the hell of the flesh trade. How can I even try to explain to you the ways in which over the last year I have indulged in illicit and immoral activities every moment! I have forgotten everything in a frenzy of sensuality and I have been busy advertising my attractions (you can call it what you like in conventional terminology). I remember nothing of my previous existence. At least I can claim a degree of success in my efforts to forget! I wallowed in the filth which collects along the river bank when the water level goes down. If somewhere in my mind I had an awareness of the dirt I was in, I tried to forget even that. Each moment of my life began to be spent in search of new lovers and I had sworn to myself that my bed would not be empty on any evening. I passed more or less 365 days and 365 nights in this manner. I was convinced that I had extinguished any possibility of married life. Now my innermost being has become so degraded and my outward beauty has lost its sparkle to such an extent that if you were to see me even once you would turn away. The stench which fills my soul leaks from every pore of my body. Previously my garments managed to hide some of life's stains, but I have torn off those clothes and thrown them away. I am as naked as the Devil! So long as only the water was dirty and there was such a stench, you could consider it to be the elixir of life. Now only the filth remains and that too has a terrible stink. I am now convinced that you would not even want to come near me!

I simply do not know how you have managed to obtain my address. In any case, your letter did not arouse any apprehensions in me. My condition is now such that you can come and see me whenever you like. Laila is no longer the Laila to whom you used to send messages of love. I have degraded my attractions in a reckless manner. My face is without vitality, my soul totally dark. Whatever lustre there is on my cheeks is thanks to powder and rouge, it is as if I am wearing a mask! If you were to see my face in the morning—I look like a witch. In the evening if you were to see me, you'd find a red painted creature of the theatre! I have exhausted my reserves of beauty. I am bankrupt and have nothing left. I have destroyed the attraction and elegance which used to drive you crazy. I have debased myself to such a degree that perhaps you would not recognise me if you saw me. Then why on earth should I mind meeting you? I have destroyed whatever was in my house. What fear need I have of thieves?

I no longer have any fear of thieves for this I am grateful to the robbers.

It really would be better if you didn't waste your time taking the trouble to come and meet me. But if you want to come, go ahead. You can spend as many nights with me as you like. You can go away having satisfied the demon of your sensuality and if after I have satisfied you, your demon seeks new adventures there are many women like me here whom I can prevail upon to cater to your lust. I am convinced that our love affair will end the moment you see me. The condition in which I am at present will cure you once and for all of your love. I have cured myself thoroughly of any equivocation which, heaven knows why, began to trouble me upon receiving your proposal of marriage. I now remember that period of my emotional shakiness with about as much enthusiasm as one remembers malaria after having recovered from fever. Come, I will also cure your delirium. When you came into my life, it was an ocean on which you sailed your boat and whose waves you stirred up with your passion. My life is no longer so, it has simply become a small cesspool in which there is no longer any water in which you can make a commotion. That vulnerability of woman which people call love and of which men have always taken unfair advantage, that vulnerability of which you saw a glimpse, no longer exists!

I was frightened by your ardour and ran away from it, and for a while remained very nervous. Even after coming here sometimes in moments of loneliness another being inside me used to threaten me by saying, 'Laila! Escape is difficult. There is still a spark in your breast which has been kept alight by love. In that old grave which is your heart, there is a corpse which is beginning to stir. What will you do now? Where will you run? In the final analysis, your beauty will have to lay down its arms before the throne of love.'

Then the devil inside me came to my rescue and said, 'What is there to worry about, Laila? You, who in a flash have reduced hundreds of wicked men to naught... Love is a snare, it is a deception, don't dream of giving it a thought. You have to take your revenge for those wrongs which have been done to you. A snake has bitten you, now ruin the whole race! Go, and poison their innermost and outward being. Your poison should be so deadly that its bitterness should permeate the coming generations forever. Don't you dare be afraid! There is plenty of poison in your sting. Crush the tiger's claw and the wolf's teeth, and victory is yours!'

Whatever my devil tells me is true. Whatever path he shows me is the right one. Sweeter than love and passion is the emotion of revenge. My devil is the god of vengeance. He is my companion and intimate friend. He is my solace in loneliness and my protector in company.

In just a few days I have made myself more secure than I ever was to resist the assault of your love. Do you still want to come? Love's counterfeit currency is not accepted at my shop, but bring as much gold and silver as you are able to cram into your pockets.

If you do decide to come—come in the way that keen shoppers go shopping. Don't come like boys who run after a drifting, floating kite. They stare at the heavens, have a piece of bamboo in their hand and they have no idea whether an abyss, or well, or a wall is in front of them because they do not look where they are going. What is the point of your coming in such a state? Make your lust your companion—your god. Partake freely in the delights of my bed, whiten your lips with the powder on my cheeks, drench your clothes with the perfume which bathes my body, and write eulogies on my false eyelashes and the colour of my eyes. Stay for one, two, or a thousand nights depending upon how much you want to spend. Be my guest, and when you have had enough, go home and marry a decent girl, and proceed at once to perform Hajj. After that who will claim to be a truer Muslim and a more virtuous human being than you!

Write and let me know when you are coming so that I can reserve a few of my nights for you!

The thirty-first letter

The letter which you have written appears to have been copied in its entirety from an Urdu magazine. These Urdu magazines sell intoxicating and delicious love stories.

After having erupted, how lifeless and cold a volcano becomes! As if it had never spewed out fire or volcanic ash! After all the mistakes I made I seem to be in a similar state; your writings of love stir no spark of warmth within me. Delicate and well-chosen words have no power to move me. I pray to God that this may also happen to you. What is known as 'adabiyat' (literary elegance) is the occupation of idleness and what a curse it is! The world of the imagination is full of lovers of all descriptions. And then there is pointless expenditure on pen, paper, and ink. God be praised! This disease is infectious; it infects both the writer and reader alike. Anybody who has two square meals day and a few moments of leisure, should read the following Urdu publication *Allama Fasih* (Eloquent Learning), *Balighul Mulk* (Eloquent Nations), *Adeeb-ul-Asr* (Writers of the Age), *Fashih-ul-Asr* (The Eloquence of the Age), *Adeeb Shahir* (Writers of Manners), *Mussavir-e-Fitrat* (A Writer of Nature), *Mussavir-e-Ghum* (A Writer of Sorrow), (Instructions on a Seaman's Verses), *Maqaalat* (Books), and *Mulahazaat Russhaat* (Intellectual topics easily explained), *Farmudaat* (Commands), *Hissia'at* (Feelings), *Nabziaat* (Pulse), *Tajaliaat* (Manifestations), *Ruhaaniaat* (Spiritual Thoughts), *Jur'aat* (Something tasteful in a small quantity), and *Ishaaraat* (Signs), and *Marmur* (Mysteries), *Zauq-e-Naza* (Visual Delight), *Fikr-e-Latif* (Pleasant Thoughts), *Afsana Ashk* (A Tearful Tale) and *Falsafa-i-Shabab* (The Philosophy of Youth), *Naghama-e-Mohabbat* (Song of Love) and *Aijaz-e-Raqn* (The Wonders of Arithmetic), over and over again and grieve over their troubles! These masterpieces can sow seeds of love even in stony grounds. The boys who read *Fasaana-i-Ashk* and *Falsafa-i-Shabaab* upon attaining maturity turn into complete lovers. Whilst lying in bed they weave endless and varied fantasies of love and attraction in an imaginary world. Then there comes a time when they desire to taste the delights of real attraction. This desire keeps increasing and every time they venture forth into the streets it gets stronger still. There comes a point when the desire becomes uncontrollable, and it is in this state that Laila's lovers fly to her balcony and keep falling off like withered leaves of a tree. Why is it that for men their wives cannot inspire love? The direction which the feeling of love takes is usually towards 'other women' outside the home. When the author of *Nakhuda-e-Sukun* and *Adeebul-Asr* sits down to write, his inspiration frequently comes from the company of women like myself. It seems as if the *nikah* kills poetic emotions. After the *nikah* no magic remains, and the poetry in the relationip between a man and a woman vanishes forever. Perhaps this is why a stolen fruit tastes sweeter—because it is forbidden. Prohibition is the friend of desire and permission its enemy!

In our literature the finest conversations are those in which the speaker strolls in the park, or performs on the stage, or is enamoured by a woman he has seen walking down the street. This is a great secret of a man's lust that until such time as he physically possesses a woman he will keep entreating her favour, but once he gets what he wants, his desire for her quickly weakens and often it ceases altogether. He reaches a certain point, and then contemplates fresh pastures. Until he does so, his emotions lie dormant within him and do not inspire works such as *Jur'aat*, *Tajaliaat* and *Nabsiaat*. The delightful portraits which appear in these masterpieces appear because in reality their writers portray some aspect of a woman such as myself. Sometimes a maiden of higher status than me is portrayed, sometimes a woman even more degraded than myself. But in this realm of imagination, very little part is played by the old mother with her dishevelled clothes and unkempt hair! It does not happen. A wife simply cannot become the beloved. It is possible that to some extent a wife may be a lover but her features do not inspire masterpieces. The literature of delight is not born from a wife. You are considered an educated and cultured young man, be fair and admit that the poetic element in your life is linked to the company of friends who seek pleasure, the writings of pleasure which you read in magazines, and the life of the streets. There is no trace of these things within the four walls of your house. The literary taste of society is heightened by the talented pen of writers of eloquence and learning, but it is our cheeks which enliven and colour their thoughts. It is our withered flowers which guarantee their poetic creation. It is our message that their talented pen conveys to a beauty-seeking world. It is the silent gatherings of women in the flesh trade who every evening advertise their beauty under the harsh glare of lights, it is these women who become a clarion call of love thanks to the understanding pen of the writer of the age. We liven up our gatherings in a variety of ways, sometimes by a glance, or by the twitch of an eyebrow, or by the hint of a smile. Your translator of reality is a turbulent lover who flails his arms around, beats his breast loudly and says, 'Come O youthful men! Love's market is open and Beauty is for sale.'

I am not indulging in misunderstanding but how many are there among the writers of these masterpieces who have not availed of the physical intimacy promoted by our gatherings? I'm not complaining. On the contrary, I am delighted that by means of these masterpieces the germs of love are being spread in every direction, and in this way men themselves are helping us to obtain our revenge. For us the revenge is sweeter when it is your own sword which beheads you, when it is your teeth which are broken and fixed to your body, when it is your poison which is mixed in your blood. Keep writing as many masterpieces as you can!

The thirty-second letter

Congratulations! You have again arrived in the valley of love, and again the thorns which pricked me, await the arrival of your feet. Again we will while away some time on discourses of love. It will certainly be an interesting occupation. I have not forbidden you to come. Come whenever you want. My house together with its contents is at your service. Apart from the proposal of marriage, all other proposals of love and desire are most welcome. I will kiss away your weariness!

The thirty-third letter

It was more or less a year ago on this day that I wrote you what I thought was a final letter. I wrote it as such ... though I now realise that that was not the case. There are still many letters to be written. A few moments after I wrote that letter, I departed from your city. Like a travelling salesman who in the morning spreads his cloth cover and sets up shop along the roadside, and in the evening packs up and moves on, I too packed up my belongings from your city and moved with my wares to a new place. The reason was that you wanted to take over everything I had! I ran away in the hope that the greater distance there was between us, the easier it would be for me to forget my humiliation and for you to forget your attachment to me. At the time I ran away my sitar was lying on top of my musical equipments and a last song waited to be played on the strings. Before my sitar could come to life, I grabbed my instruments under my arms and ran. I laugh at myself for running away like that, but I am also afraid lest I am humiliated again ... lest I should have to run from here also. But now the foundations of the fortress that is my heart are much stronger, and my sitar is nowhere near my instruments. Since you have come here searching for me, come with pleasure! When you spent the night as my guest day before yesterday, you would have noticed that a different tune was being played on my instruments. You would not have found a single part of this wilderness of my heart which is whole and undamaged. What should have happened is that upon seeing my present state, you should have left, but if you still wish to spend a few days with me, I have no problem. So far as I am concerned, apart from the pleasures of love, you will have to listen to some old lessons. If you want to waste your time, why on earth should I stop you?

Since my arrival, I have received a few proposals of marriage. My reply is the same in each case. 'My mate has just not been created by the Almighty.' But no one understands this reply of mine. A man cannot understand any way of thinking which is contrary to his philosophy of lust. In fact a man's true being has three hidden aspects, as if there are three photographs in one envelope—first, his real face, second, the self which a man thinks is his real being, and third, the way in which a man wants others to think of him. The first face is always hidden, the second face can be glimpsed from time to time by a man's practical actions, and the third face is always in front of one's eyes. I have not yet seen your true face but I have a vague idea of what it might be. However, I am very familiar with your second and third faces, how you imagine yourself to be, I know well and how you want the world to think of you, I am very familiar with. In the course of your love, you have revealed both these faces and brought them out in the open. Even if I was your wife, I could not know you better! Even on the touchstone of love, a man's true self is hardly ever revealed, but a woman, poor unfortunate if she is emotionally involved, keeps nothing hidden. I accept that like men, women too can often keep the truth hidden, and they do hide reality, in fact usually women are more skilful than men in keeping secrets. But a man defeats a woman because even in the throes of love he keeps something in reserve. A woman cannot do this. In the grip of emotion she reveals every aspect of her true being. But with a man the situation is that the woman he shares his life with, whom he makes his beloved, even that woman often cannot see the man's true face. This is the face that always remains firmly hidden. Perhaps you think that in view of our long relationship of love I have come to understand you very well, but I know that if I was to claim this, it would be untrue! This much I do know that at present you love me to the extent that, despite what the world may say about my situation, you are prepared to overlook this and make me yours. But the question remains—what is hidden in the depths of this stormy ocean? What will I find in that paradise whose door you want to open for me? I simply do not know. That is a mystery! The difficulty is that whilst I am well aware of your virtues, I am also aware of the fact that in any state, even in love, a man tells lies, he deceives, he is scheming. A man's nature is strange. He loves with genuine emotion, and at the same time deceives, and apart from the elements of earth, air, water and fire—deception and trickery are also elements which make up a man and these elements penetrate every aspect of a man's being. A man lies and deceives with as much ease as he eats and drinks. When a man truly loves and swears repeatedly to his beloved, 'O my love, I cannot live even for a day without you', he knows very well that this statement is simply not true. Every evening he says he cannot survive until morning, and then every morning he will arise hale and hearty from his bed. Again, without batting an eyelid, he will repeat these words every evening. The truth of the matter is that the more declarations of this sort pour out of a man's mouth, the more the element of exaggeration creeps in. A woman, even in love, tends not to talk much and for this reason tells very few lies. You will perhaps say that both tongue and pen are helpless before the tide of emotions, indeed in an emotional state people can even murder each other. Is this not a crime worthy of custody? I too respect emotions, and scorn those who object to emotions in life. They have no idea what life is! Without emotions what is the difference between man and machine? What is the ocean without its waves? What is fire without flame? The majesty of the sea rests on its waves, and the might of fire rests on its flames. A dry philosopher and a brainless *hakim,* if devoid of emotion, are no more than the lifeless foam of the ocean and the coal which is extracted from charred wood. If parents had no emotion, how would they bring up their children? If a man and a woman are devoid of emotional attraction, then life would become a barren waste. However, you should be aware that the might of the ocean and of the fire can bring disaster if they are excessive and out of balance. If there is no equilibrium, even a cure can become poison. You express your feelings in an exaggerated manner, and I have never been deceived by such exaggeration. If you think that the strength of your emotions has affected me in the slightest degree you are entirely wrong. Stop thinking in this way, it is simply an obsession. A woman can be deceived by a man's display of emotion, but in reality she is never overawed. But if a spark of emotion is kindled in her heart, then undoubtedly a woman closes her eyes to reality and is thoroughly deceived. She even dies of such a deception! Do not for a moment think that you can conquer a woman merely by a one-sided display of affection. No power on earth can interfere in the relationship between a man and a woman. This relationship is above and beyond the reach of the government, the law and religion; it is free from their clutches! But a man is so obsessed by the desire to own and to possess that even in love he comes like a conqueror and a ruler. But when he falls in love, a man becomes blind!

You are now again within my range. Therefore, be prepared to listen to my homilies every day!

The thirty-fourth letter

In my last letter I wrote that the mutual love between a man and a woman is totally free from the clutches of the government, the law and religion. I say again that this love is free and will forever remain so. The prejudices of religion cannot intrude into love's realm. Why do you bring religion into this argument? The religion of Muslims may have been something quite different a thousand or five hundred years ago. Today it is simply an umbrella which is used by those taking the name of religion to cater to their needs. In sunshine and in rainy weather this umbrella protects their turbans and gowns from getting spoilt. An umbrella is used as a staff to scare stray dogs in the street. In fine weather, when it is not required, an umbrella is banished to some corner of the house. Not everyone is entitled to use it. Only the purveyors of religion have the right to wield an umbrella. The problems of *Shariat* which these purveyors of religion propound, also expand and contract like an umbrella. When it becomes necessary, the issues of *Shariat* are interpreted and explained in the manner in which lawyers split hairs. Whenever the principles of *Shariat* conflict with any circumstances or worldly desires, they are conveniently forgotten or distorted beyond recognition. When any personal desire has to be fulfilled, a favourable interpretation is found somehow in some book or the other. We are then told 'this is also possible'. Why search far and wide for a view? Take a look at your own situation. Today because you want to make a harlot your wife and bring her into your house you quote from God and His Holy Prophet (peace be upon Him) and you prove how essential it is for you to give up illicit relations and get married, but yesterday when you visited my premises, where I am carrying on the flesh trade, to buy favours, you then forgot how shameful adultery is! These observations do not only apply to you; in the hands of your elders, learned maulanas, muftis and divines, the *Shariat* is a rope which expands and contracts like rubber. When the walls of madrasahs and the mehrabs of mosques resound with full-throated cries of 'sinners and outcasts', when those who stand in the pulpit or kneel in prayer, when people are categorised as infidels and graves are dug for them, when sermons are preached about what is 'superior' and 'inferior', at that time those who preach conveniently seem to forget their own 'superior' and 'inferior' points. I do not say that everyone is like this, but in this pond which is our society, there are a great many rotten fish! Many superior and inferior beings are such that in the garb of religion, they put on a tolerant face. An example is a man who, to satisfy his lust, marries three or four women. Is he not as guilty as you are when you come to see me? The only difference is that he indulges in tyrannical licentiousness under the cover of marriage. The man is the only sinner in this situation—the woman is blameless and simply a victim. The illicit relations between the two of us make both of us sinners, and the crux of the matter, as I have frequently mentioned, is a question of attitude. A man's life is a chessboard upon which a helpless woman is merely one pawn among many pieces. The man is the ruler of the chessboard. He can be checked, he can sometimes be teased but he cannot be killed. The king cannot be removed from the chessboard. All the other pieces can be removed. Similarly, with kingly force and vigour, a man conquers a woman, sometimes this conquest is achieved by wealth, sometimes in the shadow of religion.Whenever he considers it necessary, a man even uses religion to turn his defeat into victory. So, my valued friend, just don't discuss religion, apart from that you can concentrate on our relationship from every angle. I have already explained to you and will explain again that even if I was persuaded to marry you, I would ruin your social and cultural existence. Perhaps you are strong enough to take on the world, but when you encounter the fearsome glare of the religious icons, you will collapse. From childhood a fear of religion—fear, not love—is drummed into us to such an extent that our individuality is extinguished. Every breath we take is measured in religious terms, at each step we have to bow before religious tradition, and our life passes in this way. Each facet of life is intertwined with religion, so much so that our determination and intelligence are subservient to it. We are like the slaves of the pharaoh who, all their lives, lift heavy loads and endure the whip. If we breathe from the left nostril instead of the right, we are doomed to 70,000 years of punishment in Hell, if instead of our right foot we lift our left foot; we are bound to suffer 90,000 years in hellfire. If we fail to hold our nose when drinking water, fiery whips will rain on our backs in the Hereafter. If we change positions, it must be done in a certain way, likewise there's a way to be followed if we want to clean our nose, or eat, or even lie down. In short, a legal provision is attached to every breath we take, together with the punishment and its complete details! The human mind is bound on all sides and restricted in its practical application, and the development of the individual warped by these religious bodies which measure the length of pyjamas and beards and require moustaches to be weighed. Our eating, drinking, crying, laughing, sleeping, waking, walking and running are all dependent upon the purveyors of religion. Our power to choose is paralysed. Religious principles are disregarded, and life is entangled in the strictures of religion. The absolute limit is that principles are forsaken, and so are the restrictions on splendour. Love, brotherhood, humanity, prejudice—these are not discussed at all; the dispute is over whether 'Ameen' should be said softly or in a loud voice! In the same way, a woman's life is handed over to the tyrannical custody of man. When Mr Preacher sits on his seat and holds forth on problems of religion, the entire thrust of his sermon is only on one problem, namely how a wife should obey her husband. But never a word is said about how husbands should treat their wives or what rights women have over men. And anyway, the subject is not considered worthy of discussion. We women are only entitled to a handful of wheat and half a yard of cloth which the man bestows on us. The rules of our life are also made by men; they tell us what religious rules mean. They give us any explanation they want. Men have made purdah the protector of our chastity, as if a woman is so immoral that if she is not secluded in purdah, her chastity cannot remain secure. Whenever a man says that from a moral point of view purdah is necessary, he clearly means that the moral soundness of a woman depends upon him. My own feeling is that more than women it is men who should be put in purdah. If indeed purdah is essential, it should be so for men. Surely the robber who commits robbery should be arrested rather than the poor being whose house is being robbed! A woman can protect her chastity even without purdah, but men put women in purdah only because men need purdah to cloak their own sins. Despotic governments adopt various measures such as arrest, enforced silence, and many kinds of imprisonment in order to silence the voice of the oppressed. These measures are taken to ensure that the voice of the oppressed does not reach beyond the prison walls. The entire mental make-up of a man is that every action should be based on fear and threats. Fear is the biggest element in a man's religion ... and greed. The fear of punishment, and the anticipation of consequences are all that matters! A good deed is not done because it is good, but because not to do it involves the risk of punishment, and to carry it out involves the hope of reward. The human morality which rests on fear of punishment is a paper chandelier whose paper may be beautiful, but whose light is not burning!

Don't think that I have no respect for religion. But my view of religion is rather different. In my view any action taken in the hope of Heaven is fraudulent and a crime which is not committed only out of the fear of Hell, is trickery. If a sinner does not sin out of the fear of burning in hellfire for 70,000 years, the extent of his sin is not thereby reduced, his heart and mind remain sinful even though other people escape the harmful effects of his wrongdoing, because so far as he himself is concerned there is no means of escape. If good deeds are done simply in the hope of Heaven, then the good deeds of such a person have no value. However virtuous practical conduct may be, if the spirit is not virtuous, all claims of purity are false. You can form an idea of a man's attitude from the fact that the paradise he has created in his imagination is most often filled with just such delights as men consider desirable. The lowly existence of woman in paradise is confined to her becoming a houri and serving the denizens of paradise!

I don't want this argument to drag on, nor do I want to tangle with you or those who share your views. I am not irreligious, but my religious thinking is miles away from yours. The concept of religion in my mind is not that which has been explained to you by maulanas and religious figures.

How will you be able to spend your life with a wretched wife who has these views?

The thirty-fifth letter

Where have you been for the past several days? You have neither written nor come to visit. What a welcome thing it would be if your indifference heralded a lessening of your feelings! Nevertheless, I do want to know how you are, and so I am very worried because for the past several days you have been off colour. I do hope this does not mean that you are seriously indisposed!

The thirty-sixth letter

You did not even inform me that you have been so unwell that you could not pick up a pen to write a few words. And then you are lonely in this strange place. Can I not even look after you? Even if I cannot give you the degree of love which you seek from me, nevertheless I certainly am your friend, well-wisher and a grateful recipient of your favours. I simply cannot leave you alone on your sickbed. Even to this day you have not realised that you have a place in my heart and my heart is all too capable of feeling. It is quite true that I am a vulgar woman who sells her decency, but perhaps even you know that I am not devoid of human kindness. Having found out that you have been severely ill for the past several days and have not even informed me, my sinful heart received a severe shock. A woman who is capable of being a wife, is surely, before that stage, capable of being a nurse'? Do you really think that a woman, who as a vulgar lover always received your favours with gratitude, has an ungrateful heart? Do you think that she only knows how to put on airs and has no humility? Why cannot it be that in times of comfort and indulgence you owe me appreciation and gratitude, and in times of trouble I owe the same to you? Give me permission to perform this duty until you are fully recovered. This is a duty which only a woman can perform. Undoubtedly I have sacrificed my sexuality to my profession, yet even now beneath the surface, a woman still lives, who can give rest to weary travellers, who can apply balm to wounds, and who can provide a ray of light in life's darkness! Men perhaps also extinguish their sexuality in a frenzy of lust, but a woman, no matter what her condition, cannot remain indifferent to her nature, regardless of how much her sexuality maybe exhausted. I can look after and attend to your spirit. This is the dictate of my sexuality. In times of comfort and indulgence, I have given you poisoned draughts, but in moments of difficulty even I am capable of providing you with the sweetness of honey. Until such time as you return home, I will be your nurse!

The thirty-seventh letter

These four weeks have passed as if I was not in this world! I sat beside your bed from morning till night and from night till morning. Every day I created a new world and destroyed it. Nursing you was a new experience in my life. 'Thank you' for what? And who is obligated to whom? You embarrass me by suggesting that you are obligated to me. Never in my life have I nursed anyone, this was a completely new occupation for me. It is as a sister, a daughter and a wife that a woman discovers an outlet for her nature. To this day I have never been anyone's sister, daughter, or wife. How on earth would I know how much pleasure a woman can gain from being of service? I only knew how to put on airs. So far as humility was concerned, I considered that to be the province of my admirers. But during the past four weeks I have learnt some new lessons. I remembered the humanity in myself which I had forgotten. I remembered that even though I am in the flesh trade, I am a woman; during this time my soul was singing a new song ... this was a sound which I had never heard before.

Sitting by your bedside when you were asleep or delirious with fever, I used to converse with my heart for hours. My heart said to me, 'Laila, can you do even this? Is there still some genuine element left in your artificiality? You, who were used to sleeping with your hair spread over the arms of your lovers—are you still capable of staying awake in this manner by the bed of a sick man? You, who used to stay up all night in gatherings of sensual pleasure and who awoke with the dawn—can you now stay awake all night by a sick man's bed, then again all day, and again all night? You whose hands could not bear the weight of anything heavier than henna, who knew no occupation other than teasing men, each nail on whose hand took hours to polish, can these hands clean and make up a sickbed, can they support a sick man's head, and drive away the flies? Laila, where on earth did you learn all this? You who at the dead of night used to turn out your lovers who were dying for you and weeping—how on earth did you become a nurse?'

My heart would talk in this vein to me for hours and I would listen to all these strange revelations about myself in amazement.

For me this was a completely new experience in life. I, who spend two hours every morning and three every evening adorning my face and body, I, who change my outfits three times a day, wore the same set of clothes for five days at a stretch during your illness and was not bothered by them being crumpled and soiled. I never thought of washing my face all day. None of my admirers will ever believe how I managed to pass four weeks in that way.

When a woman loses her self-respect, she regards herself as degraded—that feeling is like death. If a woman feels this way, even if she survives, she does not live and feel as a woman. If a woman should suddenly in this state feel that despite every degradation, there still remains a degree of womanliness inside her, that she is not yet as wretched as she thought she was, then she once again awakens from her mere existence. A glimmer of life in a deathlike existence is something to be thankful for. After these weeks of your illness I have begun to feel as if there is just such a ray of light in my benighted existence. This is something I had not imagined in my wildest dreams! It is as if I have accomplished something, as if my affections have been compensated. Then why on earth are you thanking me? Whatever I did was out of my affection. Why then do you insult me by thanking me?

The thirty-eighth letter

When you are dreaming of palaces and suddenly find the humble hut in which you live on fire! When your imagination is transporting you to the summit of a mountain, and suddenly you find yourself in the gutter! When you are convinced that you are considered as being one of the famous and renowned writers, that your place is in the ranks of learned and outstanding men, that each word you have written is treasured as if it were a diamond or a pearl and all at once an old postman from your street delivers a postcard from the editor of a journal, which says, 'I regret to inform you that your article is not worth printing.'

When you imagine that you are a renowned leader of the community and accorded the highest degree of respect; you imagine that your neck is weighed down by garlands, thousands of people are pulling your car, your spellbinding presidential address has caused a sensation, and that with every breath you achieve something unique and then suddenly you awaken from a deep sleep to find yourself lying on a tattered mat in a drug den!

When the force of your intellect clothes you in the garb of religious learning and you find that in the courtyard of the mosque and the madrasah, thousands are kissing your hands, and prostrating themselves at your feet, when the hem of your gown is considered to be the covering of the *Ka'aba*, and the entrance to Heaven or Hell is dependent upon a mere lift of your brow, when angels from highest Heaven are bringing messages to you, and then suddenly you are rudely awakened by the noise of heavy iron doors banging shut and you remember that the police has charged you with the offence of absconding with a woman of ill repute and you have been arrested for that.

When you dream that you are a famous flier and have taken your plane to the summit of Everest, and that newspaper columns are full of your achievements—then you suddenly wake up and find that instead of an airplane, a drifting kite is landing on the roof of your house and you run to catch it...

When you dream that you are riding on an elephant or in a car and find yourself in an *ikka*! When you are dreaming of a tiger's prey and the bite of a mosquito makes you jump up from sleep, when you imagine delicious and delectable food being fed to you, and see only a dry crust of bread in your hand, when you dream of the grandeur and majesty of a ruler and on waking find yourself to be of a stature no greater than that of a slave—at such a time you realise that the difference between a dream and its interpretation is *indeed* a difference.

When I sat by your sickbed during the darkness and silence of the night I used to dream that I was a respected and decent wife looking after her husband. This dream was so pleasant that I forgot the stress and trouble of staying awake at night and nursing you. Some nights passed so pleasantly that from evening until morning as you lay there, delirious with fever, I remained in the realm of dreams, but now I have ceased to nurse you and have come home! The routine of lovers and their declarations of love has started again! Once more a crowd of lovers who are dying of the pangs of separation is gathering. Now I am realising how bizarre dreams and their interpretation can be. Someone is saying to me, 'Laila, the world of the sick man you nursed is not for you. You don't belong there.'

The thirty-ninth letter

You, now by the grace of God, seem to be to joining the exalted and august company of writers. When you perceive yourself as capable of writing lies, which have other lies concealed within them from which in turn innumerable branched lies can issue, then you can rest assured that you have become a writer! The hallmark of a writer is that he is impatient to see his name in printer's ink. If journals and newspapers indulge in a criminal intrigue and neither is prepared to publish a particular writer's articles, he can find other means of publicity to counter these unreasonable and unjust moves. In other words he can start issuing testimonials to chemists to enable them to advertise successfully. From hair oil to the invigorating elixir of life, he can write down his experiences of each medicinal preparation and send these to the owner's factory. Without doubt such writings will be published, and his spirit will be satisfied with the renown which will attach itself to his name. No matter whether he has actually used the invigorating oil or not, yet he would write, 'I was absolutely bald, but this invigorating preparation made such a lot of hair grow on my head that now every third day I have to call the barber.' Whether or not he has ever used body tonic, he will boldly state, 'I lost so much weight that I weighed merely a few ounces! During my student days I was so thin that if I sat sideways in class, the teacher used to mark me absent. But after drinking this tonic, I am ready to wrestle with *Maulana Shaukat Ali*.' About a particular preparation, he will swear, ' ... its properties are such that the dead come to life and often have done so in various places!' He will then proceed to produce a lengthy list of his ailments and will write—'All the *hakims* and doctors had given up, but this miraculous remedy got rid of all my ailments. It is as if I have been born again thanks to these preparations. I used to have backache, my eyes watered, I had painful rheumatism in my legs, my kidneys were very weak, there was a swelling on my liver, but this amazing remedy has made a sixty-year old a new man. I feel a surge of youth in my veins, and want to gain admission to college once again!' This certificate will be published under the title 'Marry Four Wives' which will have a full-page advertisement and will be carried by serious newspapers and journals. This is the way to get even with editors who are unreasonably pernickety in publishing articles by writers. What I mean to say by all this is that if you really want to become a writer, then you should model your articles on advertisements—the models of which should be in front of you.

If the large-hearted editors of newspapers and journals are not prepared to publish these letters of ours, and if our love affair cannot come to light in any other way, then the details of our relationship should be published by means of an advertisement by a chemist shop. You can issue a certificate that will state, 'This miraculous remedy completely cured me of love's malady.' I will issue a statement to this effect, 'I used this intoxicating compound preparation in accordance with a special prescription and it was so effective that I was forced to abandon my immoral activities.' Then just see how our names will feature on the pages of newspapers and magazines. People will ask, 'Who on earth is this Laila who, as a result of taking this intoxicating compound according to a particular prescription, became a decent woman? And who is her lover who was able to escape from the clutches of love by taking this miraculous remedy?' People will then search me out and come to my house. Among them will be many flies who will get stuck in my syrupy sweetness. On one side will be the proclamations of repentance, on the other the subjugation of my lovers.

> *I continued to be a drunkard, yet never let paradise out of my clasp.*

Rather than writing letters, it would be better if you could start writing the story of your unsuccessful love affair in some Urdu magazine. Such a move will benefit me, and you will also start receiving proposals from high-ranking families to be their son-in-law! What is the point of wasting your literary talents in writing anonymous letters? If you want to make a name for yourself in the world of letters, learn to compose advertisements.

The entire reason why I am writing this letter is that these days an editor and a major pharmacist are entangled in my web. Perhaps the reason for the editor being enmeshed in my web is because his skill as a writer of articles is stimulated by my attractive manner and it is possible that the pharmacist has been captivated by the hope of finding many buyers of his invigorating preparations in my house!

The fortieth letter

Dashed hopes and longings, faltering determination, wavering enthusiasm, stale thoughts, stale kisses, worn-out love, both sorrow and happiness equally worn out ... my whole life ... a tired story ... Oh God! In these circumstances, why are new worlds of longing stirring in my weary heart? Longings which are compounded of happiness and sorrow, which jostle and struggle with each other creating a tumult in my tranquil life. I am like an insect which is born in the soil, lives, eats, and grows in the soil, and one day is crushed into the soil by the foot of some traveller. Is this wretched insect totally unaware of what will happen if desires stir in its breast? The brightness of the sun, the light of the moon, the beauty of the flowers, the flash of lightning, the roar of thunder—none of these elements can stop longings from entering the insect's breast or end any longings which have stirred and disperse this handful of dust throughout the atmosphere!

You must wonder at my mood swings. How strange they are. Sometimes I flash like lightning, sometimes roar like thunder, sometimes I rain and go on raining. Sometimes I whirl like a rising storm, sometimes I smile like a flower and sometimes I weep like a dew drop. In the midst of laughter I weep, and I laugh in the midst of tears! There is no consistency in my nature. Now a cool breeze is blowing, and in an instant there is the searing hot wind of a summer afternoon. I am in a strange state; an odd human being. Who has made me like this and why is my nature thus?

You tell me that it would have been better if you had continued to remain ill so that I could have constantly looked after you—but when did you recover? Ever since you and I met, from that day to this, it has seemed to me that your mind has been ailing, your heart is sore, your breast wounded, and from the beginning of time, I have been your nurse, not just your nurse, but your physician as well. The treatment I am giving you has sometimes taken the form of wit, sometimes contempt and dislike, sometimes anger, sometimes love, sometimes tears, and sometimes laughter. You are incapable of being abstemious, that is why you do not get better. You do not give up what is forbidden, you have become irritable like a long-term patient, you throw tantrums, you do not seem to realise that nursing is much more difficult and stressful than illness. Supposing I were to be ill, and (God forbid) develop your illness, would you be able to nurse me? Will you be up to it? How can I make you realise that till now you have not seen anyone who is really ill. You don't know what illness is. When you develop a headache, you consider yourself ill. It is when you bathe in sweat and your body feels as if it is breaking up, when your insides burn with an intensity that will melt iron and your eyes dissolve in tears, then, consider that you are ill. At the moment, you are simply out of sorts, that is all! You are not even aware that the only people who are alive in this life full of longing and wistfulness are those who die of yearning and those who suffer illness. The rest are simply walking corpses! You have never seen ill people. When the point of a lance pierces your heart, when the razor-sharp blade of a sword enters your soul, when a poison-filled arrow enters your body and is a constant torment ... then consider yourself ill!

The forty-first letter

Sin? What did you say? What do you call sinful? Why should something from which no human being can escape, which is so widespread throughout the universe that it involves one hundred and one per cent of humankind, be considered wrong? If it is a sin to drink water, to see with one's eyes, to hear with one's ears, then please tell me whether there is anything at all which is not sinful? Who is there who does not tell lies, who is not faithless to their own species, who does not forcibly possess property belonging to others and is not ready to die for every inch of land? Who does not fight with his own brothers for the sake of a penny piece or for every mouthful? Who is such a person? From a king to a beggar, from the tallest minar of a masjid and the biggest bell in the mandir to a two-penny prostitute—who is such a person? There is no such thing as sin or virtue in the world! The foundation of human life rests only on two elements; power and weakness. To be powerful is totally virtuous; to be weak is totally sinful. These are the only laws, the only religions, the only rules of conduct, the two principles of humanity, the two balances of the scale. The two words 'power' and 'weakness' encompass all the details of human life. The powerful make laws, the weak receive punishment. The powerful erect tall monuments to their fame and strength, the weak merely dig their graves. Drinking is entirely permissible for the powerful, but for the weak is absolutely prohibited. A murder committed by the powerful is fair and justifiable revenge, whilst that committed by the weak is punishable by death. Any unnatural act of the powerful is regarded as naturally correct, while that of the weak as one that deserves punishment! For the powerful to behave in a tyrannical and oppressive manner towards women, is both necessary and appropriate, but if the weak behave in like manner, all hell breaks loose. There is nobody as sinful or full of ill deeds as a weak wretch. When two thousand women and girls fill the harem in the palaces of the powerful, these women are all begums, and all of them are obliged to obey their master, but if a weak man has more than one woman in his house he is immoral and wicked. The most violent murderer, who is licentious and a drunkard, can become *Amir-ul-Momineen* (leader of the faithful), *Khalifat-ul-Muslimeen* (Leader of the Muslims), and a Maharajah, but punishments are meted out daily to the slaves of such *Khalifat-ul-Muslimeen* and Maharajahs, for murder, licentiousness, and drunkenness by the courts of these high and mighty personages. Punishment and reward are not at all dependent on either good or wicked deeds. In reality, it is the power or weakness of the parties concerned which determines punishment. This being the case, why on earth are culture and standards of behaviour exalted to the heavens when there is no justification for doing so?

You will argue that without the present system, human civilisation cannot survive, my point is—Is our present civilisation so indispensable? Was the world not inhabited by human beings without it?

If the balance between the powerful and the weak is based only on physical force this undoubtedly will be a process of natural selection. But when at every level of society, between every two people, even though they be father and son, there is competition and this competition is based not on physical strength but on cunning, deception, and trickery, when these qualities become the basis of superiority, then how is this world any less than hell? When we can live happily or unhappily in the hell of this world, why then should we fear that other Hell with which we are threatened by religion? My feeling is that the other Hell is perhaps less painful than this one. At least in that Hell there will not be the politics of the powerful crushing the weak of the same sex! In our world, those, who have developed the art of enslaving and trampling on the rights of others, are considered high-minded. The process by which one nation swallows up other nations in its capacious stomach is what is called politics! Society consists of a wealthy and cunning stratum which can rule over all the other strata of society and by fleecing them, increase its power. If truth be told, in our social set-up, from the time of the Prophet and Noah, people have always been divided into two groups. For instance the Brahmins and the untouchables. Muslims, Hindus, Christians, Parsis, Persians, and Arabs—all are subject to such a division. The Brahmins are the rulers, the untouchables the slaves. Ruler and ruled, Capitalists and workers, maulanas and their murids—behind these different screens, the reality is the same and the reality is hidden! The powerful and the weak, the bad and the good, sin and virtue, holy and unholy, high and low, believer and infidel, ruler and ruled, master and slave—all these are technical terms coined by the powerful and it is by this criterion that the weak are categorised. If today you become weak, and I powerful, your very existence will be an unpardonable crime, and my carrying on the flesh trade will be considered a decent act! My actions will be regarded as being attractive and permissible, whilst whatever you do will be hailed as sinful and a crime. Those contemptuous and humiliating glances would be cast at you, which today I have to endure. Your greetings would be spurned, whilst my car would be pulled by admiring throngs! The difference between your actions and mine is not worthy of attention, it is in fact the difference between power and weakness which has placed a woman's neck to be crushed beneath a man's foot. When God created the world, did he intend our lives to be governed the way they are today? Because you are more powerful than I am you are bound to argue that the existing system is the essential and true aspect of nature. I will have to accept your behaviour. But remember that this is not what I believe. In comparison with the powerful, I am weak but I am a rebel! You can strip me of my humanity, you can assault my decency, you can install me in your house as a serving woman, but belief is the one thing which the powerful cannot snatch from the weak. God-given nature is the most secure shelter of the oppressed. Man by his power and connivance has wiped out woman's individuality. He has put the mark of slavery on a woman's forehead. But he has until now not managed to wipe out a woman's convictions. In India, and probably all over Asia, women will one day launch a terrifying revolt against male domination which will shatter the complacency of your selfish society. You and I will probably not be alive to see this rebellion, but that storm will have the force of the flood of Biblical times! Our future generations will see women taking over the thrones of men, and revenge will be taken on the oppressors for their oppression. There is little doubt that the day of judgement will be a harsh one for cruel men!

Whenever you don't like a woman's behaviour, you say it is sinful, it is a crime. But if we ever even presume to object to any sin or crime of yours, you are ready to gouge our eyes out! Women of the street, like myself, are the most deeply wounded and the most oppressed. It is women such as myself who, God willing, will stand in the front ranks of the rebels and put the point of our spears on your chests and say, 'Return to us everything that you have robbed from us over the past centuries, account to us for every drop of blood that you have spilt, compensate us for our unfulfilled hopes, dashed longings, wounded hearts, and shattered fortunes. Count each wound which you inflicted; they are still green. In return for each wound, your wicked spirit will be bound on a criminal's tripod and given one hundred thousand lashes!' On that day your arrogance will be broken, and the scales of God's judgement will be evenly balanced.

Thousands of women like me are dreaming of revenge, your oppression will increase, and it will swell the ranks of the rebels until one day the powerful and the weak will exchange places.

You may well laugh with contempt at these idle thoughts. Carry on! Go ahead and laugh! Humiliate and debase a woman's vulnerable existence! Yet this laughter of yours will one day become a noose around your neck and strangle you. It will be a taste of Hell and it will stick in your throat.

This is my reply to the insinuations in your letter about my sinful conduct ... do you want to hear anything further?

The forty-second letter

In a small locality there lived an old woman in a broken-down house. One day she had an urge to cook *kheer*, so she sent her child to the market to buy milk. The child was returning home with the milk when he spotted a kite drifting towards the earth. Several boys were running towards the kite, trying to grab it. The child also ran, and in the process the earthen cup of milk fell from his hand and broke into several pieces which remained on the ground. A little later, the son of a rich nobleman raced his car along the road, and a sharp piece of the cup pierced and punctured the tyre of his car. As a result, he had to wait a while in the small town to get his tyre fixed. Whilst he was doing that, his eyes fell on a beautiful young woman standing in the archway of a house in front of him. He fell in love at first sight, and after forming an acquaintance with her parents, in a short while, he married the young woman. Seven children were born to the couple and each one of them later had a family of their own. The future generations founded a tribe and within a century peopled various small towns.

How this slight wish of the old woman led to an increase in the world's population! If that day instead of wanting to cook *kheer*, she had simply cooked *khichdi*, neither would she have sent her child to get milk from the bazaar, nor would the tyre of the young nobleman's car have been punctured; neither would he have married the young woman from the small town, nor would there have been seven children and seven new families.

The wife of a nobleman had a very sharp temper and was very stubborn. The nobleman too had a temper which was liable to flare up in a moment. At breakfast time, the maid accidentally dropped a pat of butter in the drain. The lady of the house was furious and slapped the maid. The maid complained to her husband who in turn brought the problem to the nobleman's notice. The nobleman, who was already angry because he had not got any butter with his breakfast, punched the maid's husband, and so hard were the punches, that the man's spleen burst. The nobleman was arrested for murder and sentenced to seven years' imprisonment. His wife died of grief. The property was auctioned to pay his debts. Today there is no one to remember the nobleman and no one to light a candle at the grave of his wife.

A small event had a momentous result. Had the pat of butter not fallen in the drain, perhaps this family would not have been ruined.

A handful of dust, an ant, a mosquito, a twig, a little water, a leaf, a thorn, a small wish, a little anxiety—anything can be the prelude to great events which may have significant consequences. In the ordinary course of things, an unimportant incident can often have a frightening result and lead to a bloody revolt. Kingdoms are destroyed, and thrones toppled. For instance, a bird flies off a tree with a seed in its beak. Whilst in flight over a barren wilderness, the seed falls out of its beak on to the ground. A gust of wind covers the seed with a handful of earth and a few drops of rain fall upon it. After a span of fifty years or so, miles of dense forest cover that barren waste and it becomes a haven for birds, deer and predators! Who can know why and from where the first seed fell? Look at the difference between the beginning and the end of this chain of events!

How fascinating and frightening is the sequence of cause and effect. Just realise that causes arise with every breath we take. The causes are so infinitesimal that we are not even aware of them. But the effects can be such that whether manifested in a day or a hundred years, they will fill many pages in the books of history. All those pages record a small event as the starting point of greater things. Even a historian does not know the source of the events he is writing about. Just think how obscure our life is, how few options we have and how far beyond our understanding and perception it is! But we claim (and men more than women) that we are aware of everything.

Think about our relationship. What a tiny coincidence it was that one evening when you attended a gathering at my house, just because of shortage of space, you sat next to me. Then again, by a small coincidence, my lighted cigarette fell from my fingers on to the floor; you picked it up and gave it to me. However, if on that evening the room had not been so crowded, if my cigarette had not fallen accidentally from my fingers and if you and I being strangers had not exchanged a few words, how would the tumult which has been besetting our lives for the past two years have arisen? God knows where you and I would have been. You had no intention that evening of falling in love with me. For my part I was at that point looking for admirers. You had attended many such gatherings and I had already advertised my attractions on many such occasions. At that time I was completely new to this life and not entirely familiar with the practices of this profession, so there was no reason for me to have remembered you. After our brief meeting that evening, I was for several days involved in my profession. The very next morning, in fact even before the gathering had dispersed that night, I had forgotten who you were, but the seed which some feathered creature flew away with from that gathering lay for a while on the barren ground and you and I were oblivious of its germination. Somewhere there was a gardener who kept tending to the seed. We had no idea, but it kept growing in the field of life. Today its branches wave in the wilderness. Where there was not a breath of wind, today there is a strong breeze blowing. Who knows what is to happen? Will love and affection flourish or will the flames of disappointment and despair engulf the forest? Who can predict whether you and I will spend our lives under this shady tree, whether we will build a home among its branches, or whether some day there will be a violent storm that will uproot the tree which will then fall on top of us and our crushed corpses will be covered by its leaves ... who knows?

You'll keep on singing tunes about your love, I'll keep singing about my beauty. Whoever is making his move on life's chessboard, will place the pawns as he pleases. What can we possibly know about it?

The forty-third letter

It is good that you have gone. It was only right that you should go. You were also quite right in not meeting me before your departure. When I say farewell to friends I become a coward. The fact is that I run away in fear from everything which pains my soul. This is a weakness of my character; I am frightened at the prospect of facing distress. When a situation is about to arise—one which I consider will cause my soul anguish, I try to run away as far as possible, and if such a situation does in fact arise, then I create new occupations for myself so that I can banish the memory and the pain from my heart. I absorb myself so completely in these new occupations that there is no scope for any reminiscence even in my imagination. I close all the doors of memory like a lone woman who bolts all the doors of her home at night for fear of thieves. Despite all these precautions, sometime or other a thief does manage to enter my house, and when this happens, the entire evening (if I am alone, otherwise several moments) passes as if each breath were my last. Many many nights and days have passed in this struggle! I am still alive, many travellers come to my lodging, they stay and move on, some come back and there are even some who want to make this lodging their home. You too are one of those. I don't know whether or not you are aware of the fact that I fear you; your existence seems frightening to me. When you are in front of me, it seems as if a thief has entered my heart. I feel my steps faltering ... my mind and heart seem to be going astray. When you leave, a blanket of fear is lifted from my heart. I realise that there is danger, but it is far away! I am in a strange state. I fear living in the river, yet I become anxious at the prospect of the bank. In the river is the crocodile, on the bank, the tiger and wolves. In which direction shall I go? Where shall I go, O God!

At night when my client having exhausted his lustful urges goes to sleep, my eyes scan the dark room for a spot of light, my ears long for a song of my forgotten youth, I am always fearful and despondent, always waiting. I hear the sleeper's snores, but I am away from him in my own world. Sometimes I am in search of life, sometimes death. In the stifling silence and darkness a clock in the niche in front of my bed sounds a constant refrain, 'Finished ... finished ... finished ... youth finished ... luxury, youth is over. Hope is finished. Life has ended. All is over ... all is over....' The voice of love, which spans the beginning of time to this, and that bliss which dwells in a woman's soul—all finished. Sometimes the loud snoring of the sleeping lecher mingles with this refrain of the clock, 'Finished. Finished. Absolutely finished.'

Morning comes, I hide my ravaged face and rush into the next room lest the wretched man's mood should be spoilt on seeing me, then I out of exhaustion go to sleep. I have no idea when he wakes up and goes home. But when you sometimes come to spend the night at my lodging, the refrain of the clock changes. It no longer says 'Finished! Finished!' but 'Tomorrow, tomorrow, tomorrow ...' All night this continues. This refrain gives rise to a meaningless fear in my heart. Someone whispers in my ear, 'What will the morning after this dark night be! What is to happen tomorrow? What is to happen tomorrow?'

The traveller who stays the night at my hostelry and departs in the morning writes 'Finish' on a page of my life and goes away, but you ... but you ... you fighten me, you sow fear in my heart! All night I tremble and in the morning I cannot escape from your clutches. You do not write 'Finish' on the page of my life, you go leaving all the pages scattered and I remain, trying to collect the scattered pages together.

I am glad you have gone. Consider your preoccupation in love to be guaranteed by your correspondence. Write to me from time to time and I will reply,

The forty-fourth letter

Someone was knocking at my door. Who wanted to enter my house at the dead of night? Why did they want to come in? Who is it that wanted to come in? What did they want? Where had they come from? Who was it? Who was it?

From a corner of my bedroom a naked form was coming slowly towards me. I was trembling in fear, I was drenched in sweat. My customer, in whose arms I was lying half-naked, was in a drunken stupor; he could neither see nor hear anything. Drops of sweat were dripping from my forehead, and that naked form kept coming towards me.

'Oh, who are you? Are you blind? Can't you see I am undressed? I need privacy ...'

A soft sweet voice replied, 'I am an angel. I have been banished from Heaven, I have rebelled against God. The guards of Heaven have been commanded not to let me set foot there.'

'Why have you been banished?' I asked him. 'Why have you come here?'

'When I was brought before God's court, there were other angels with me, who were also accused and we were all presented. We said, 'O God, we cannot endure your independence and cannot accept your absolutism; you ask for nobody's opinion and keep on doing whatever you wish. If matters go wrong, you do not do anything, we can no longer tolerate your independence, give us a share in your kingdom.' God's favourites and flatterers said, 'O Lord all these are your angels who have become rebels. They want to have a share in your heavenly kingdom. They have hatched a rebellious conspiracy against you.' The following command was issued, "Throw all these angels out, banish them to the world where women exist. These beings are compounded only of fire with which some clay should be mixed. Take these rebels away. Tell them to add a little clay from the world to their constitution. Let them go to some woman. She will sort them out properly.'

'And what happened then?' I asked in amazement.

'Then we were flung out of Heaven, our wings were pulled off, our resplendent garments were torn off, now we are in search of that sex which is called woman. Are you a woman?'

The tone in which the naked angel spoke was like a gentle breeze which makes the leaves of the chinar tree rustle. He kept coming towards me repeating the same question, 'Are you a woman?' 'Are you a woman?' I was collapsing with fright. He put a hand on my shoulder and I began to tremble. Then he asked again, 'Are you a woman?' In a terrified voice I replied, 'Yes, I am a woman.'

'Mix some clay into my fiery composition, oh woman, I have rebelled against God,' said the angel.

I started to play a forgotten melody on my broken string. 'No,' he said, 'This is a heavenly melody. You do not require this. I am tired of listening to it. Play me an earthly tune.'

I picked up a broken string of my instrument, sat on my haunches, and began to play. The angel put his head in my lap. A melody began to emerge from the broken string, at first, soft and slow. The air in the room began to tremble and the angel started to sway. 'Yes, this is it ... Yes, this is it,' he went on saying. 'Keep playing, keep playing woman, keep playing on your broken string. This melody is much better than heavenly music. Much better ... The sarod is more delightful than paradise. The sound from your broken string ... Keep playing.'

I was no longer frightened; I was absorbed in the melody from my broken string. Sometimes the angel would roll in my lap, sometimes on the floor. There was a fragrance from his body which I had never smelt before! I don't remember how long this state of affairs lasted or how long I continued to play and he kept swaying in time to the music. I have no idea. All I do remember is that the muezzin of the local mosque was reciting the azan for morning prayers, when a spark flew out of that writhing body and a voice spoke out of the flame, 'Oh woman, you are mine ... I will come again.' I shut my eyes.

This morning, I was repeating this extraordinary event to myself and thinking that it would not be surprising if man, who claims to be the ruler of woman, is not in fact a rebellious angel banished from Heaven. When man arrives on earth, he joins the ranks of the Devil's forces. Is it only woman who can cure these rebels of their rebelliousness? Was no cure for these hot-headed rebels possible in highest Heaven and must they come to ruin this habitation by becoming a garland around a woman's neck? Is our sole purpose to keep adding our clay to their fire? If only we had been asked to perform some other task! If only we had been given responsibility for other duties and had other pastimes! Why are rebels sent from Heaven into our laps!

The forty-fifth letter

Why do you complain to me that I have forgotten you? I have not forgotten you ... nor can I ever forget you ... a woman does not forget. It is only when a woman forgets she is a woman that she ceases to remember. Every event and circumstance, whether trivial or serious, is locked in her heart.

The farmer's wife who collects manure all day from dirt tracks, takes the sheep and goats to graze in the fields, and bathes the oxen at the village well ...

A poor widow, or a poor married woman, who scrubs dishes, grinds masala and cooks roti ...

A poverty-stricken, helpless old woman who sews clothes for payment, and kneads *ata* to fill her stomach ...

A maid, who for five rupees a month, looks after the children of the well-to-do and sells vegetables ...

The female teacher who teaches children; the begum who lives in palaces; the lover of gold and jewellery, brought up in the lap of luxury; the woman of education and skill, who writes articles in newspapers and magazines; a half-baked follower of Western culture, who like a gilded butterfly flits about in gardens among flowers, and like a lamp bestows her tasteful glances on men in gatherings and assembles ...

The political woman ... Shrimati devi ... who wears khaddar and delivers speeches ...

The actress who every evening displays her various talents to the audience ...

And Laila, a woman of the street, who is part of the flesh trade ...

... all these women will remember each pebble and each particle on life's stony path and they will only forget when they forget their womanhood. A woman's life is bitter just because she cannot forget, a man's life is more relaxed and assured because in the morning, he easily forgets the doings of the previous night! All night he indulges in constructing habitations of love, and in the morning he kicks down their walls and goes on his way. In fact, a man by nature is a nomad while a woman worships a particular place. A man makes any place his home and enjoys himself. A woman stays put in a particular spot and finds it difficult to leave; she only leaves from there in her coffin. Even if she does leave that place, she remembers the place all her life! She lives in gardens, she adorns gatherings, she beholds storms at sea, she passes through barren wildernesses and in the end comes back to the spot she has been searching for. She just cannot forget until that sleep overcomes her which is capable of making one forget everything in the world.

There is a major difference between the nature of men and women. A man doesn't think deeply and doesn't try to understand too much. He never remembers. He is intoxicated by the feeling of being the master and doesn't think it necessary to examine a woman's nature too closely. Two great religions of Asia have forever made women slaves of men. This being the case, why should men waste time finding out state of their slaves? After all, a slave is but a slave. The disciple asks his guru, 'O guru, how should we treat women?'

'Just don't look in their direction, Anand.'

'And if in spite of every precaution, we cannot resist looking at them?'

'In that case Anand, don't talk to them.'

'And if, O guru, we do talk to them?'

'Well then, Anand, watch out for yourself.'

And the lawgivers of another religion have said, 'The curse of God be on this sex, you are the path of the Devil, you destroy the image of God (in other words you destroy men).'

Islam has given women some more rights, but after a short while the rulers of Islamic kingdoms seized them and even after the first half century, Muslim women became the victims of men's all-embracing oppression. I want to collect examples from all religions so that I can show you how for the past five thousand years one half of God's creation has been enslaved by the other half. Countless women have been destroyed. Man considers himself to be the image of God and considers woman to be the path of the Devil. In the ocean of life, women are the rotten fish!

If only men, who least deserve to be considered as examples of learning and graciousness, would spend a few moments examining a woman's nature ... just a few moments ... which are free of the long-held prejudices of revered writers!

The forty-sixth letter

There are three different types of people and they have three different attitudes:

- *This is what should happen.*
- *This is what has always happened.*
- *If only ...*

The person who is successful in worldly terms is he whose aims and desires are based on the maxim 'this is what should happen'. He has a focussed strategy and before he takes any action he resolves that 'this is what should happen'. He is not concerned with causes or impediments and is indifferent to consequences. His sword is unsheathed to spill blood, and he says, 'This is what should happen.' He desires to obtain worldly wealth, to conquer nations, and his motto is—this is what should happen. In the realm of learning and excellence, he receives tributes from people. This maxim he regards as the basis of truth. He exercises sovereignty, he founds new kingdoms, he usurps crowns from others—the sword of generalship is tied around his waist—he annihilates nations and peoples and when the world regards his conquests with wonder and awe, he listens to eulogies and songs in his honour with supreme indifference, and he rationalises each fresh success by saying, 'this is what should happen'. Whenever he says 'this is what should happen' he achieves his aim, and he is indifferent to any prohibition. Like a flood, he surges on and on and he sweeps away everything before him. He wreaks havoc and destruction on the earth and in grand style collides with the ocean.

But he, who at every stage says 'this is what has always happened', in comparison to the flood which collides with the ocean, is like a small pond in some village in which the same few frogs live which have always lived there. On the banks of the pond the same few oxen and the same few pigs come to drink as they have always done. The filth of the area keeps flowing into the pond, but the pond doesn't mind, filthy animals come and bathe in its water but it doesn't care and after each incident it merely says, 'This is what always happens,' and accepts the situation. The pond never complains. It isn't even aware of reality. A man such as this has no sensitivity or perception; he is neither pleased by success nor disheartened by failure. He simply does not know the difference between the two.

Does he whose blood runs cold in his veins and who does not have the vigour to draw his sword, know how stimulating a wound can be? No desires or hopes trouble him, no resolutions or thoughts torment his tranquility! He is a living corpse and thinks that it is only the act of breathing which is the basis of life. He is full of such complacency that his sleep is not disturbed by the promise of the morning and the newborn day brings him no gifts. His silent world is indeed like a pond. So far as he is concerned, the pebbles cast into the pond by village boys, which create a few ripples on its surface make the pond an ocean.

He always stills the restlessness of his spirit by saying, 'this is what has always happened'. This mantra of lack of action and lack of awareness dampens his soul. He is unconcerned about more or less everything and is free of worries about the future.

More alive than either of these two kinds, but nevertheless forsaken, is he who with every breath says, 'If only!' From the day of his birth till his last breath the refrain 'if only' keeps him involved. 'If only, if only ...' echoes from all sides. He could explain his entire philosophy of life with these two words. They could define every morning, evening and every moment of his life. He need not search for his destination or the tranquility and comfort that reaching his destination would bring. He may wish for a continuous and never-ending journey ... he may wish for activity and may not require a beginning and an end. He may always want a beginning and a continuation. His life would be a continuous refrain; there would be continuous activity! He would always be occupied. He would build and demolish. Should rivers run dry he would fill them with water; should fields dry he would keep irrigating them, should hopes elude him, he would still cling to them, should determination flag, he would revive it. He would keep stumbling and yet pull himself up! Even if his courage should sometimes wilt, he would keep reviving it and upon each desire he would say, 'If only things could be like this!' He would seek to ascend from the earth to the stars, and even higher. He would never sit still. Even if unsuccessful, he would still aspire for success. He would not rest content with 'today' but search for 'tomorrow'. In his creed, contentment, the restrictions of life, the calm of death, desire and searching are the treasures of life!

From top to toe I am one of those who say 'if only' and you are completely in the category of 'this is what has always happened'. If only you could be transferred to the category which says, 'This is what should happen!' If only the power to search had been aroused in you, then our respective powers of will could have competed and some day your case and mine could have been decided.

So far the taste for enquiry which you have exhibited is an empty one. It contains tears, sighs, several laments, complaints, and nothing else. With one disarming smile, I can still all your demands. When your demands will not be stilled at any price, then you can consider that you are free from the chains of lust!

The forty-seventh letter

The owner and manager of a theatre, who has been longing to meet me and often comes to my house, got rather drunk yesterday and began to insist that I should become the main star of his stage. With his slurred speech, he sketched delightful vistas of fame and renown before me. Each evening thousands of fans would be enchanted by my talent and I would become famous. To whichever city the company would go on tour, I would be able to leave an impression of my skill and fame. Within six months I would be a household name in the whole of India and God knows what I would not be able to achieve in my lifetime. My beauty, my dancing and musical skills would set a new standard in world theatre and my fans would tour every corner of the world singing my praises. I would, by virtue of these eulogies, become the moon if I were a mere star, and if I were the moon, I would become the sun and so on.

He said all this and much more besides! I explained to him that his 'art' was on a different plane compared to my sinful existence. I told him, 'Good or bad, I have made a stage in my premises for myself. On this stage of mine I put on various acts from morning till night and I am quite confident about the success of my venture. This being the case, why should I sing and dance on your stage like a puppet under glaring electric lights?'

I do not have strength for patience.
The tyrant has sapped my will.

Why should I neglect my own melody and sing yours instead? Why should I turn a blind eye to my own dance and dance to your tune? I am by birth an actress and my talent is no less than yours. My coquetry and my narcissism still generate an adequate income. What more do I want? I am still not short of the praises and commendation of worshippers of beauty. My 'conquests' are still considerable! Then if I set aside my highly placed admirers who are in effect my slaves, in order to cater to the coarse tastes of those who sit in the lowest seats and dance about on wooden planks—who is more stupid than myself? My actions may be worthy of censure, but I am not without taste! I can write better drama than your well-known dramatists who write vulgar and obscene plays. Don't ask me to act in a drama, ask me to write one. There have been so many dramas played out in my own life which continue on a daily basis, that if I were to commit even some of them to paper, the owners and managers of acting troupes like you would be jolted out of your composure. Commerce is an independent profession, I wish to remain independent. Why should I give an average man a share of my income? The whole point of your scheme is only that you wish to promote my attractions as an agent would do!' The poor chap was very embarrassed and with a shamefaced laugh changed the subject!

You must have seen many women acting and dancing on the stage. As a matter of fact, a woman's whole life is lived on the stage. Have you ever realised that in our society a woman is obliged to put on an act from the time she is born until she dies? All the time she keeps acting in accordance with the directions of the 'master'. She follows whatever directions her husband, father or brother may impose on her. There is just no question of independence, conscience, or intellect. When a girl grows up within the four walls of her house and arrives at the age of adulthood, she becomes the focus not only of her immediate family, but of those connected with it, so that her getting up, sitting down, waking, and sleeping—in short—her every action is according to the wishes of such an audience. When a husband is found for her (everything is found for her—she cannot choose anything for herself) she leaves one house and has to put on an act in another house. Her father-in-law, mother-in law, sister-in-law, and brother-in-law—all form the audience. She is sacrificed for these people both in regard to her life and death. If in terms of India's somewhat dubious conventions, she is 'educated', then the ambit of her acting is widened to include meetings, parties, conferences, bazaars, parks, and that circus which is called 'society'. In this case, the stage and the theatre are just larger. How difficult it becomes for her to act when she is aware that her feet are shackled by the rules and regulations made by men and she has to take each step in accordance with the wishes and intentions of men! You will argue that a woman is happy in this condition. Yes, undoubtedly. If you rear a fledging parrot in a cage, feed it, and teach it to talk just as you wish, keep the cage door closed and the food and water of that parrot is under your discretion, then in such a case the parrot will not know how to come out of its cage and even if you open the doors of the cage and free the bird, it will keep flying around within the walls of your house, because the strength of its wings has been taken away. If you then say that this parrot is free and can fly about wherever it wishes, it will be nothing but specious tyranny on your part. The fact of the matter is that men have assumed control of all the grace, power of action, and potential that is within women and over the past centuries have slowly but surely established such complete dominance over a woman's nature that a woman is no longer able to understand the true meaning of independence. The few women who are demanding independence mistakenly confuse outward manners with independence. The inner capacity to think, the independence of ideas, the independence of mind is real independence. Until women are able to think and understand things on their own, without the help of men, and to work out for themselves a way of life, and by their own intelligence able to deal with the problems of life, and in the light of their conscience decide the course of their future, they will not be independent. At the moment, woman is being deceived. Men are teaching women to go about dressed in elegant saris. They make women learn all those pointless songs, which are the composed by and played on the instruments of men. Men encourage women to be 'educated' and then teach them to make the same meaningless speeches as they do themselves; they teach woman to be patriots and reformers just as they are themselves. And men claim that they are giving women independence! All this which is being given to women is counterfeit currency. A woman is being made into everything but is just not allowed to be a woman! Women are clothed in beautiful saris, driven in grand motor cars. They attend magnificent gatherings and conferences in splendid palaces and they are put in prominent positions. The men are reassured by their arrogant conscience in the following terms, 'All these women are your slaves, their fame is actually your fame, if they are a celebrity you are a celebrity too. When these women attend large gatherings, elegantly dressed, and their bodies are bedecked with jewellery, it is your name which is taken. Your wife, your daughter, your sister—all of them are your puppets. Make them perform, give them everything except the independence of spirit. Keep that door closed, but open every other door. Let them become independent. They will still be subservient to you.' Men are championing the cause of womens' liberation. Hundreds of newspapers and magazines have been launched to promote the reform and progress of 'the fair sex'. Thousands of speeches are delivered and resolutions passed on this subject, as if men are proving their independence and liberal mindedness to the world by these gestures only as if to say, 'Look we are giving women their rights.' But if you were to go into the homes of these loquacious speakers and prolific writers, you would not even see a glimpse of those articles, speeches, and resolutions on women's progress. When a wolf comes into its lair, it discards sheep's clothing and assumes its true form. The man who on the public platform beats his breast for womens' rights, at home starts beating his wife. In public he pronounces that womens' rights are equal to men, but when he comes home in the evening, if there is too much salt in the food, he flings the plate at his wife's head. This is the deception practised by the deceivers! Men know very well that so long as women remain intellectually subservient and consider themselves as the 'weaker sex' they will not escape from the control of men. I would tell all my sisters and particularly those who are no longer in purdah, who consider themselves liberated just because they make speeches and have become 'leaders' of the community, that we, poor unfortunate beings, will remain subservient to men until such time as we liberate our intellect and absolutely and unconditionally refuse to accept that men are superior. If we can develop the power to refuse, then we will acquire all the ability to act. Until this happens, all this talk of women's progress, liberation and rights is mere child's play.

I will take my own case ... when at the beginning I left home and came into this profession, I had a strong sense of the graciousness of men; the same men who defiled my innocence, who degraded me, who used to laugh at me—I considered myself beholden to them! I was ridiculed by the sensuality of men, they used to make fun of me and all along I put up with this humiliation by thinking that this is what I deserve. Even after suffering from the wickedness of men, I used to consider myself even worse. But the experiences of life opened my eyes. Today I consider that in spite of my immoral practices I am still a human being and the weight of my sins is far less than that of those committed by predatory men in comparison to whom I am more honest and have an innocent conscience. I am a sinner, not a fraud, men are more sinful, more dangerous, and more wicked than I am! The blackness of sin is stamped on a man's soul, on my soul there are blood stains and running wounds; my heart trembles with the fear of God, but his heart is in the Devil's clutches and all he is afraid of is worldly disgrace. His actions are only sinful if people manage to find out!

The oppressed party at a certain time becomes aware of oppression; many of my fellow women are thinking about the end of tyranny. You will perhaps object—you always do—and say to me, 'You are full of talk but you provide services to those very men whom you consider oppressive and wicked,' but as far as I am concerned, your view is not correct. Whatever I do is in the context of my profession, but in my mind, God be praised, there is no effect of man's superiority. I dance in my theatre only in order to feed myself but I give the men who come to watch such contemptible treatment that they will never forget. I regard as lower than sweepers those admirers of high rank who come to my premises in motor cars. I experience a strange satisfaction when they make impassioned requests and succumb to my attractions. I treat their overtures with contempt and I am happy to do so. I humiliate them in every way possible and tell myself, 'You beast, this is just what you deserve and you should be humiliated further.' They pay the price for my favours; I consider them as fuel for the hellfire in which I find myself. When a new admirer is entangled in my web, I feel like saying, 'Come, O my prey, I shall roast you, the flames of my fire are very fierce. Lie on these coals; the more your blood sizzles, the more refreshed my spirit will be.' These customers do not pay me for my favours, in fact they even sacrifice their humanity. They must think that they have achieved a great victory. I, for my part, think that I have soiled the spirit of a beast of this world, that I have annihilated it, and put a mark upon it which cannot be erased. In truth, the victory is mine!

The day I cease my activities, whatever the reason for my doing so, that day I shall become a liberated independent daughter of Eve, with only one aim in life ... to reduce the superiority of men to the smallest particle. I will devote my entire life to achieving this objective.

If, with these thoughts and intentions I become your wife and enter your home, will you allow me to continue my struggle? God knows that for me the sweetness of revenge is infinitely preferable to the ties of marriage!

The forty-eighth letter

I haven't written to you for quite a while. I could not write. A change seems to have come over me. These days I think a lot and don't say much. Sometimes, it is as if the page of a book has been turned and it gives me a start! Your assessment is not wrong—I am subject to swift changes of mood. These days I am in a state of ferment and restlessness. I have no idea what kind of tumult this is, why, wherefrom and how it has arisen. There is a force—eternal and perpetual—holding my reins and there is a faraway voice which is calling me, which is guiding me. It is as if some long-forgotten melody like an ecstatic surge originating near the rainbow touches me and a new quivering of life stirs in my innermost being. It is as if one's finger touches live electric wire; I feel a series of slight shocks. Of all changes of mood which I am experiencing at the moment, the strangest is that my lost youth, which I never cared about, is becoming dear to me. From the time when I entered this profession I have been squandering my youth and my beauty with both hands, I have scattered both generously among my throngs of admirers and I have tried to ensure that the number of my admirers constantly keeps increasing so that the sooner I can get rid of my beauty, which is a burden to me, the better. The sooner the edifice of my attractions is buried, the better. But God alone knows what is happening to me. In some remote recess of my being there is a wish to preserve safely whatever little remains of my physical beauty. Someone is whispering in my ear, 'Laila, take care of whatever is left. Some claimant is going to come and ask you to account for everything which you have recklessly thrown away; preserve whatever you can. When this party, who is going to come, will say to you, "What have you got for me?", then tell me, what offering will you be able to produce from your ruins? When a conqueror conquers your town, will you have some tribute to offer or not? Or will you appear wretched and poverty-stricken in his presence?'

I have given away countless flowers from my garden. There is a small flower bed in which a few flowers remain. Now I have an urge to ensure that these flowers somehow flourish and don't wither! Perhaps this is the first indication that old age is approaching. After having squandered golden sovereigns I have an urge to put away the few remaining pennies and keep them safe. This desire has arisen just as poverty is knocking on my door. My own condition is similar. As long as I had an abundance of wealth, I squandered it recklessly.... Now when all the wine I had has been thoughtlessly drunk and only the sediment is left in the cup, I want to preserve this at all cost. What explanation is there? I can neither say nor understand anything anymore. In the verdant vale of my life, the branches are bare, the blossoms have fallen, my youth is disappearing like the wind.

Why do I want it back? Why do I run after it? If this is not a sign that the period of youth is ending, a sign often visible in people, then what on earth is it? Perhaps the voice I hear is the voice of truth. The sexual attraction which I offered to brighten and illuminate my trade, I now want to change into a gift of love and offer to someone who comes along ... and when he does ... that ruler of love's kingdom ... then I can place this humble gift, my beauty, all its potential charm, my youth, my music, my songs, all my capital under a velvet covering and offer them to him with the words, 'Oh my lord, this is a tribute of love from me, a poor beggar woman. Accept it as such. You have come belatedly when my entire city has been destroyed! Whatever is left in my treasury is yours. After this I have nothing left.' I am in a state of wonder. Oh God, who will that person be? When will he come so that I can offer him my tribute in this manner and hope that he will accept it on these terms? Who will he be, for whom I am keeping my parched fields watered? For whom am I doing this? For whom? If only someone would tell me! Why do I hear the sounds of life from the bell of death?

The forty-ninth letter

I used to employ fewer words but their meaning used to be greater. You used more words, but they had very little meaning. Now I am using many more words, but my thoughts are in a tangle. Your words have become concise, but your meanings are numerous! You are changing somewhat, I too am changing. Does this mean that one day you and I will change places? Or will you and I meet at some central point? What will happen then? The day that you swore you would give up physical relations with me and would instead learn to love, in the way that love should be expressed, that very day, I too resolved that if you kept your promise, I would try to take a few steps towards you. You constantly ask me whether or not in my opinion you have proved to be true to your promise. At the moment, I cannot make any comment except to say that from the time you decided to banish sexual indulgence from our relationship, I have found a new pleasure in your friendship, I sense a new feeling. The shamelessness which arose out of our immoral relationship was a huge obstacle to our spiritual existence. From the time our immorality ceased, the obstacle has also grown less and less. Now when I meet you I no longer perceive the stench which earlier I found so repulsive. During a flood, the water of a river is dirty but when the flood recedes, the river is clean once again and the water becomes fresh. Now when the flood of your sensual desires has receded, clean water has begun to flow in the river. Does this state of affairs portend a mighty tumult? Will the tumult occur in my life, in yours, or in both our lives? God alone knows. What is the consequence of the transformation of our relationship from an immoral to a chaste one? What change is taking place in the shadow of our sinful conduct? Assuming that you really raise yourself up to a higher level of being, will you also be able to pull me along with yourself, out of the mire? Who knows what is to happen but such a possibility is certainly a very pleasant thought for me. When an eagle clutches a dove in its talons and soars into the sky, can the wounded dove, terrified and imprisoned in the eagle's talons, also be happy? For the dove, height means extinction. But perhaps I can accept even this. If perpetuity is denied to one, extinction is not such a bad alternative! In my present state, there is neither perpetuity nor extinction! I am stuck between the two. If life is not granted, what is wrong with death? In my present existence, in which I am neither dead nor alive, my actions deserve death and extinction, yet I retain a desire to live. Somewhere far far away, in the depths of my soul, there is a desire for perpetuity which resembles a fluttering flame, and outwardly my condition is one of tumult! That dying woman, that woman who yet lives within me, even now in the quiet of some night, in the solitude of some day keeps whispering slowly and softly to me, 'Laila! Your wine has turned to vinegar, your sweetness into bitterness, empty your cup and fill it with a new kind of wine ... Hitch your destiny to a new star ... you are a woman ... a woman ... not a plaything! Keep alive in your heart that jewel which is a woman's inheritance. You are capable of love, you can be loved. Fill your lap with the gifts of nature. Burn every shred of your outward clothing and offer your innermost nakedness to the threshold of love. That is your place, that is your home! You are a woman ... a woman ... seek your mate, and make a place for yourself, a place where even in death you will live. You are imperishable!' I miss you, come!

The fiftieth letter

What can I write to you ... I am very busy ... come and have a look! I am mending the planks of my broken boat, sewing the sail, repairing the rigging ... It is as if a violent storm is about to break ... Which sailor will come and rescue this broken boat? There is no wind, the atmosphere is still; I am watching the gathering clouds, and my gaze is on the flashes of lightning. The wind is about to blow, the waves of the ocean are getting larger. Someone is pushing me and my boat towards the waves saying, 'Get into the boat. Cut the ropes. The saviour of your boat has come.' I ask, 'Where has he come from? Will he come wrapped in the storm? Will he come on the shoulders of the clouds? Will he come wrapped in the folds of the waves? How will he come? Where will he come from?' But a voice keeps saying, 'He has come, he has come'. It doesn't listen to me and keeps on saying the same thing.

The fifty-first letter

So you have found me again! I simply don't have the nerve to face you. I would rather die and become extinct. Do me a great favour, get away from me and leave me alone. Let this gilded butterfly flit about in gardens, if you touch it, the colour will come off its wings. No one is listening to me ... someone is coming towards me! My eyes are sleepless and await the sunrise. My boat is ready, and the lap of the ocean is inviting ... my sailor has come!

Your crops will be irrigated by my blood. In order to adorn you, I will be destroyed. The dirt in me will be cleansed and pure after touching your feet. In order to lay a foundation, the earth is dug, rubble and slime are collected in heaps, planks of wood are broken and cut to size, bricks are crushed. It is only after all this destruction that a mosque can be built. Out of this rubbish rise the arch and the pulpit. My mosque is ready, but how can I, impure as I am, set foot in it!

After a storm that lasted all night, the day is dawning. Autumn had stripped the trees bare of leaves but spring is furnishing them with fresh garments. Along with these garments, comes a new pleasure in life. Will my autumn too receive the promise of spring? Will the broken-down walls of my barren life be rebuilt? Why are these flames leaping up in the darkness within me? Who is it that is sitting like a king upon the throne of my heart? Is it you? You did say to me, 'You can keep running from me, but I will by stealth and in secret, find a place in your heart. You say you are unable to love me. I will teach you how to love.' You have acted on your words! I used to say, 'The man destined for me has not been born. My mate has not come into the world.' Today, my man has come, my mate has come, I am his and I live for him alone, my life is his, my leisure is his. He, whose existence I used to deny, and he, to whom my spirit called, has come. You have come to me!

The fifty-second letter

Those who are attracted by superficial matters have begun to review my letters. They think that whatever is written in these pages is the story of my life. How short-sighted—and a man's short-sightedness at that! What a terrific joke!

Not even an iota of my life is contained in these pages. I merely existed—I had no life that could become a story. I have only just woken up from a long sleep. The woman who has lived within me and has been asleep for the past twenty-five years is now opening her eyes and stretching.

These fools have mistaken her first stretch for the whole story! They have mistaken the beginning for the end! Reams of criticisms and reviews have begun to flow, merely on one tiny instance of reality.

I am writing to dispel misunderstanding. All this is merely the introduction to my story. An account of awareness will now begin after a brief account of a dream. I am now fully awake and if I survive in the embrace of love I will write something about what a woman has to go through. My male readers in their anxiety should not consider the starting point of my life as the conclusion!

Let me live this new life for a while, a life whose doors are beginning to open for me. Let my barren existence bloom. The time for me to have my revenge upon criminals will be when as a wife and a mother, I shall raise the banner of revolt. At the moment, I am just a woman of the street, disgraced, humiliated, with my head hanging down. I will ruthlessly expose all the so-called polished manners and civility under the covers of which men tyrannically exploit women. I know only too well that these scoundrels will say—'Laila! Is this the same Laila who until yesterday evening was in the flesh trade? She earned her living from us and now has the cheek to taunt us? Has she become the embodiment of purity and chastity?' You will make a face and taunt me, and I will laugh and call you to account for all your wrongdoing. I have not put the words 'the end' on these pages. In fact I am going to make my conclusions the title of a new volume.

A few words of truth from a woman of the street have made you so angry. But when you hear these same words from a well-bred, modest wife, what will you say? Truth cannot be silenced simply by ridicule and humiliation. These are the weapons of frivolous and shallow people, which are always blunt and without effect.

Oh yes, wait for me in another life!

—*Laila.*

Majnun ki Diary

Extracts from Majnun's Diary

Author's Explanatory Comments

At the time when Laila's letters was published and read with great interest, my friends often felt the need to point out to me the extreme candour with which Laila expresses herself. This candour was considered by some people to be too extreme and beyond the limits of decorum. People even said that Laila's habit of playing with the emotions of a Muslim who embodied religion and humanity to a supreme degree and her coquettish behaviour was absolutely unacceptable. I repeat now what I said to my friends at the time:

> *It matters not how often the truth is discussed,*
> *Unless it is expressed in appropriate terms any discussion*
> *is without effect.*

The manner of expression used in *Laila ke Khutoot* was the only appropriate and suitable way to relate the story I wanted to tell. Laila's story concerned the subjugation of women. In the social milieu of India, such a subject could not have been discussed by any decent well-bred daughter or wife. There was no option but to have these shameful truths revealed by the pen of a woman of the street. A sober and decorous narrative would have robbed the issues discussed of meaning and effect. I wanted a sharp thorn to prick the thick skins of those upon whom a normal pinch would have had no effect. The constraints of sobriety and decorum often blunt effectiveness. In truth, I was compelled to use Laila's pen as a means of puncturing tough, thick skins!

How far I have succeeded can best be determined by those who have read *Laila ke Khutoot* not merely for their literary flavour, but who have been aware throughout of my main objective. The spirit of my story is revealed by Laila's flowing pen. Her story can be regarded as a few drops of blood on a wounded woman's shroud. The letters reflect some imprints of those wounds. This 'Diary' is also an attempt of the same kind and is a pen portrait of a modern young Indian. I have attempted to reveal some aspects of a young man's innermost and deepest feelings. Neither Laila's letters nor the diary is a mere literary exercise. Praise from those who read these pages superficially and view them as having literary worth, and who fail to understand the essential importance of these portraits—I do not regard as worth having. As far as I am concerned, the approval of such readers is simply misguided approval.

Lest my words be cast aside as a mere exercise in self-conceit, let me add that I have not written a single word of the 'Diary' as an exercise in penmanship. My protagonist is a wealthy, educated young man carefree, playful, who in every state of being, whether crying, laughing, angry, frustrated, on the point of death, in love, in sensuality, drunk, in the company of friends, in the brothels of Bombay, in lonely evenings, while consummating his love, in conversation with the stars, or with religions figures, or in playful teasing ... whatever he writes on any of the above states, anything he puts down on paper, illustrates his innermost condition ... That tumultuous condition which has ruptured the framework of his life. In short the point is that these pages seek to portray various objectives and truths.

In order to portray the innermost truths about a person who has broken with every religious, social and emotional convention, the style of expression too has to be appropriate. There are times when sobriety of expression robs the aim of its point, and often the truth has to be demonstrated by calling a spade a spade.

After this preamble, let me state my topic. In this modern age, those young men who are considered educated, and free from life's struggles, are able to indulge their emotions and feelings to the fullest. They become totally ignorant, indifferent and oblivious of the ordinary Muslim. They create for themselves a new world based on total ignorance and lack of awareness. Along with this half-baked state which in our country is called 'education' young men are increasingly veering away from their centre of gravity. Their priorities don't exist, and a frightening degree of confusion has arisen in their lives. Without correct values, an education in which the learning of the East and West remains disordered and incomplete, produces either human beings who like animals somehow or other manage to grab two square meals a day and then perish, or young men alienated from both intelligence and religion, who consider that the sole purpose of life is to pander to basic emotions and indulge in unbridled hedonism. Such young men are deprived of religion's guidance because the preachers of religion take no notice of their condition nor have they the capacity to do so. These stewards of the truths of the *Shariat* have no idea why there is such an enormous difference and remoteness between the generation of Muslims who were born thirteen hundred years ago and the present generation growing up in a world of revolutionary change. They reply ... these religious leaders of ours ... that whatever has been written is correct. If that book was written six hundred or nine hundred years ago can it be that it continues in force despite the passing of centuries? The door of analytical thinking is closed! There can be no analysis even of a broken *lota* in a mosque. The world may change beyond recognition. The power of the human mind and of science may turn men into robots and change the contours of life itself. But what is written will remain in full force and effect! Western education has revealed new concepts to young men. Their acceptance of these concepts means that they cannot strike a balance between modernity and traditional beliefs and in the end they become misguided. The self-deception and self-importance of religious figures easily turn these young men away from religion, and they are like boats at the mercy of a violent storm with wild winds and waves, on the surface of which they blow about like cotton seeds. On the other hand, there is Western education which is available to young men and whose consequence is that it can produce BAs, MAs, doctors and scholars, but is unable to produce human beings. Everything can be gained by this education, except education itself. This education consists of a few pages of history ... that too, not our own ... a few pages of geography, a few exercise books, a few principles of science, one or two books of English literature, one or two Urdu, Persian and Hindi journals. This is the prescription, and the systems of these young men are filled with its medication. Then these young men are given a black gown to put on their shoulders and a flat three cornered cap to put on their heads. This is how these new soldiers are prepared to confront the struggles of life. Whose fault is it? Whoever is to blame, it is certainly not these poor young men. They are so ground down, dissolved, and sifted by the colleges they attend that when they leave those colleges and schools their eyes have no vision, their minds are blank and their backs are bent! They catch it from both sides. The religious element labels them reprobate and accursed and shuns them and the world does not allow them to earn their living. Harried on all sides, these young men either regard the shortcomings of the religious element to have been produced by religion, and become either atheists or agnostics, or they regard all the faults of their teachers as a product of the system and rebel against the present socio-economic system. They try to start afresh under the banner of socialism. They are free from worldly and social inhibitions, and recklessly give vent to their confused emotions which activity they consider to be the prime object of life, and destroy their lives in an orgy of excess.

The portrait that these pages reveal is of the innermost feelings of one such young man. One particular point is worthy of note. The revelation of character analysis is that which is evident in every word and deed of the protagonist. He does not accept the rules and standards laid down by others. In every sphere of life, whether it be politics, manners or religion, he judges everything by his own criteria, and doesn't care one bit for what others think. This reckless and unbalanced attitude pushes him in all directions and does not allow him to find contentment anywhere. He accepts no restraint upon his sensuality and wishes to indulge his every desire, he wishes to get the best out of life, but give nothing in return. He wants success; he wants to fly without effort and without wings. When many of his desires prove impossible to attain, he is frustrated, and in his anger, sometimes attacks the arches and pulpits of religion, sometimes assaults the pillars of culture. This is the young man's state of mind, this is his essential being, this is the struggle in which he is engaged, he is aware of his limitations and is even prepared to confront death. In an attempt to show his freedom and independence and to confront death, he propounds a new doctrine of suicide. He declares war and rebels against the old-fashionedness of life. The short-sighted regard him with contempt, but they only see the outside. They are unaware of the tumult that is raging within him. If whilst reading these pages you can read between the lines you will easily realise that in spite of the banner of revolt which this rebel holds aloft, sometimes there is a flash of real worth in his life, just as there is a flash of a glow worm in the darkness or in a dark corner of the forest. Towards women for instance, he unashamedly propounds his selfish sensuality, but when a streak of real feelings disturbs in his sensuality and indulgence, then this rebel against the world senses a shock, and instead of advancing steadily to do battle for his cause, he suddenly stops. The splendid cover of his sensual independence hides a weak spot. There is a spark of real worth which still remains hidden in some dark corner of his heart. But the purveyors of religion are on one side and the standard-bearers of the intellect are on the other ... Neither of the two cares at all about the spark of real worth; in fact they are simply concerned with superficiality and on this basis form opinions and issue judgements. The physician treats fever and changes his prescription several times a day. Neither does he search for the underlying cause of which the fever is a mere outward symptom, nor does he have the competence to do so. Then when the patient just does not improve, he wonders what the matter is. He doesn't even consider his own lack of intelligence, and he blames the patient!

I am not too hopeful that these pointers of mine will suffice to arouse sleepers from their slumber. But if deafness afflicts hearers, this does not mean that the speakers should be dumb. This is merely the beginning of the discourse. The story of *Laila ke Khutoot* and *Majnun ki Diary* still remains to be finished, and future instalments of the story will be presented in due course.

Abdul Ghaffar
Hyderabad Deccan
12.07.1934

18th February 1929

I went to bed at five a.m., woke up at two p.m. in the afternoon. All night I watched dance performances and kept on drinking steadily. If one does not drink at a gathering of one's friends, then indulgence loses its zest and becomes a tame affair.

Who was that creature who was sitting next to me last night? I hear that she is someone new who has recently arrived. She is fairly attractive and seems to be very young. There is a girlishness about her face, and how shy she is! I tried for hours to get somewhere, but in spite of my efforts the young lady just would not converse frankly. What shyness and reserve! My view is that she is pretty cunning and crafty. Her shyness was actually an act. The cigarette which fell from her fingers was a premeditated move so that I should pick it up and pay attention to her. God preserve me from the wiles of women. What sugar-coated pills they are—bitter inside, sweet outside; their cat's claws are sheathed under soft fur—I have seen plenty of them! What a fool Sunder Bai[3] made of me. What a hard time she gave me ... and Bi Mushtari too ... What bitter draughts I had sipped for two years ... What a set up! Keep shelling out money, keep up the flattery, and listen to abuse, put up with tantrums, be made a fool of in public and weep and weep until you finally die. But nothing that one does has the slightest effect on these hard-hearted creatures, God preserve us from these female sirens. Now one has to wait and see what this Bi Laila is all

3. Sunder Bai, Bi Mushtari, Bi Laila by names of courtesans

about! She sits next to me and says nothing—the poor thing just doesn't open her mouth! A lighted cigarette fell from her fingers on the floor ... as if this was just a coincidence! Oh yes, tell that to someone else! I am not such a fool. She dropped it on purpose so that I would pick it up and attend to her. I am well-versed in such tricks. She bends her bow towards Tom and the arrow strikes Harry in the heart!... I also have to find out more about her. At the moment she has only caught my fancy, Mir Sahib told me that she has only been in the city for eight days—but I have no doubt that she has mastered all the tricks of her trade. Only the angels of Hell know the truth about these corpses but whatever be the truth, she is not at all bad! I noticed last night that there were quite a few chaps who were seeking her attention. How greedy men are and as far as women are concerned, men never seem to have enough. Whichever woman is available, wherever she is available, will do. If nothing else, he can feast his eyes on her, and after all, apart from delighting men, what else is the point of a woman's existence? The 'desire' is that of men and women are the 'desired'. After all, flowers from the garden are also gathered because they are beautiful and fragrant, and their kind is always 'desired'. No law or religion can curb natural instincts. These instincts are always free and will remain so ... a man will be a man and a woman will be a woman ...

25th February 1929

I sent Mir Sahib to Laila's house and told him to find out how matters stand. Am I likely to succeed with her or not? Am I going to be led a dance and be exhausted in the process? But Mir Sahib told me that she hardly deigns to say a word and when she does talk, her words carry a great deal of weight. It seems that she is fairly educated. When Mir Sahib arrived, she was occupied with her studies. He just kept sitting there. She kept studying. When he brought up the subject of her meeting me at the gathering and reminded her about the incident of the cigarette, she said, 'Oh yes, I do seem to remember that there was some gentleman sitting there ... I am a stranger and a newcomer here, and apart from anything else, I am not particularly interested in meeting people. If the gentleman would care to come to my humble abode, let him do so.' My word! What airs! I told Mir Sahib, 'You are an absolute idiot, being frightened by a mere woman! All this seriousness of hers is just an act, oh Mir Sahib, you should have made your intentions clear and settled matters. It isn't as if she is a prince's daughter. She is what she is, nothing more.' Mir Sahib replied, 'My dear fellow, I was in a sweat ... her manner was that of a well-bred woman. When I summoned up the courage to tell her "your beauty is the talk of the town", I cannot tell you what a face she made, as if she was talking to some pimp on the street. "What do you know of beauty?" she asked. "Beauty for you is like casting a pearl before a swine. You men only recognise your lust ... you have no idea of the beauty of others. What you call beauty is skin-deep. It is only beneath the skin that true beauty exists. Please talk about some intelligent and civilised subject." After listening to this lecture I was flabbergasted,' said Mir Sahib. 'What more on earth could I say?' 'Oh well,' I replied, 'I have to see this side of her also. Let her come one day, and let steel clash with gold ... this philosophising will come to an end.'

12th March 1929

What a lot of toing and froing! At last, she visited me yesterday evening. Whatever one may say, the woman is intelligent and interesting. Her conversation was so analytical and well-reasoned, that I was amazed. Then there is her beauty and her youth! I was captivated by her attractions and even went so far as to say that she should visit me every evening. But the hard-hearted creature gave me a blunt reply, 'Oh yes, if I were to be at your service every day, what would be the fate of my other admirers? I am a joint property—the attendant of an inn. I make the bed of any traveller who comes to stay; I cook their food. If I were to leave my inn and take up a position outside, what would happen to my guests? If you are a well-wisher of mine, then I will certainly come and see you from time to time. She laughed as she talked, but there was something in her laughter ... as if she was in pain. She laughed like an invalid. God knows who this woman is. She is definitely not from the common rung of such women. When I wanted to question her further, she got up and swiftly departed.

14th March 1929

I called her several times—she didn't turn up. She said she was busy and didn't have the time. I wrote her two or three letters and received this reply, 'If I had the time to write to you, would I not have come in person to see you?'

She does the strangest things. My friends taunt me. 'So you've started to wobble—you've become a marshmallow. Do you want to get entangled?' they ask. These people simply don't understand why if a man likes a woman's company it should be considered love. Love is a vulgar meaningless convention. It is in reality another name for lewd and meaningless sensuality.

God! This so-called poetic love is a hellish problem. In heaven's name the real element is woman, and a man's natural desire for her. If any friend of mine comes and says to me, 'I am crazy about a certain woman,' I tell him plainly, 'Have your head examined—you seem to be very short on good sense. Or go and commit suicide instead of bothering me.' Akhtar *Mian*[4] was once crazy about a girl and came to see me bemoaning his condition. He then dissolved into floods of tears. I told him, 'You idiot, have you gone loony? If it is an affair that you want, have it for some months with a woman who is easily available. If you wish to express your love, do so like a decent, well-bred human being—why weep and wail if you can't succeed with the woman? Buzz off from here. Either your digestion is upset or your liver is afflicted.' That day, Akhtar *Mian* was very angry with me, and until the day he was involved in this affair, he remained annoyed. When the affair had cooled, he came to see me. He laughed in an embarrassed way and said, 'Oh my dear fellow, do forgive me. What a devilish tangle I was in. That girl gave me such a hard time. Anyway, the matter is over. I now hear that she is getting married. The proposal first came to me, but I said, "For goodness sake what has love got to do with marriage?" I then sent a message to say, "You marry whomever you want. My love will not be able to survive the chill bonds of marriage."' He continued in this vein and then said, 'I hear that a new creature has arrived. You have struck up a warm equation with her. I too have a share, my friend.' 'Have you gone mad?' I asked him, 'When I myself have no share where is the question of yours? She is a rather strange woman ...'

21st March 1929

What an awful day I spent! Maulana Khairuzzaman Sahib[5] dropped in God knows from where (every pestilence is sent from

4 One of Majnun's friends.
5 A religious figure who is an acquaintance of Majnun.

the sky), and when he did arrive, he became a fixture like the Qutub, and pearls of wisdom began to drip unceasingly from his lips. It was as if one was tied up beneath a leaking roof! As usual, his store of advice and counsel was opened; this is wrong, that is a sin, this is a weakness, this a strength, Hell, the angels, Munkir and Nakir! In a word, his stroking of his beard and his endless pontificating irritated me excessively. He said, 'Young man, now that you have reached adulthood try to examine your conscience. A sinful existence is intoxicating at first but eventually it destroys one. My dear fellow, (this is the maulana's pet phrase—my dear fellow) how long will you continue to be negligent?' Then God knows how many *ayats* and Hadith he started to quote ... I am sick and tired of the word sin; it seems as if sin is all there is in life. Sin! Sin! Sin! Whether one sleeps, wakes, eats, drinks, laughs, weeps or talks—it is all sinful. A drink of water is sinful, it is sinful to eat, in fact, whatever you do is sinful. Maulana is wholly virtuous, I wholly sinful! Finally I got fed up and said, 'Sir, do not open the basket of your religion before me. This is all a bag of tricks. I just do not accept your meaningless babble. Whatever you say, kindly be good enough to give me an explanation at the same time. You say that for a man to go near a woman out of wedlock is prohibited. Why so Sir? Only because religion has decreed a law about the relationship of men and women and has dumped that on our heads? What is there in marriage except offer and acceptance? But if there is offer and acceptance between a man and a woman which is not expressed in conventional religious terms, in such a case why are sexual relations between a man and a woman not allowed? Suppose that a person just does not believe in your conventions and your religious nonsense—why do you stuff your law down his throat? If someone rejects the very existence of the Hell you speak of, what effect will reciting '*Khalidina-fee ha abda*' have upon him? Maulana, I maintain that man is made for woman and woman for man, not because religion regards them as each other's garments, but because it is a natural impulse for men to be attracted to women and for women to be attracted to men. This is a basic fundamental and straightforward fact of life, which religion has tangled up terribly.'

'If you are so governed by natural impulses even Nature has decreed a balance. Try to observe that,' replied the maulana.

I said, 'Certainly, if one exceeds the limits of balanced behaviour, Nature itself punishes us. Why do you have to shove Heaven and Hell into everything? Since when have you become qualified to pronounce on natural impulses?'

'Religion encompasses Nature, and I am a representative of religion,' said the maulana.

'Indeed Sir,' I retorted, 'What a religion, and what representatives it has! You have distorted and disfigured the whole scheme of Nature. In its place you have erected a new framework of inheritance. To maintain this framework, you have decreed rules and regulations for spouses. You have shackled the natural instincts of man and woman, and have suppressed wholly natural impulses. What has been the result? Natural impulses have started to compete with religious strictures and both have become each other's enemies. Natural impulses are being fulfilled in secret; hypocrisy and artifice, like serpents and scorpions, are slithering and thriving in the folds of religion. Whilst this goes on you have nothing better to do but argue your head off about what is permissible and what is prohibited! In the meantime, the impulses of Nature, have by skilful tunnelling escaped from the custody and chains of religion. Man's animal instincts are normal and natural. By declaring them to be outside the limits of human behaviour, you have ended up beating an empty drum. You have erected ever new regulations of abstinence. A natural human instinct has been shackled. What a system!'

The venerable maulana looked at me aghast and smiled but I said whatever I felt like saying. 'What kind of system is this Maulana! Nourishment is before you. How easy and natural it is to pick up and eat. But you have set up a thousand rules which prevent this, such as—take the first bite like this, chew in this way, gargle in this manner, wash your hands in this manner, belch like this—normal natural functions have been enmeshed in hypocrisy. Something which was easy has been made difficult. This is religion for you!'

The maulana said, 'You are out of your mind. If you don't believe in religion, at least believe in your intellect.' I replied, 'Sir, woman was the captive and the possession of man. Nature made man her lord and master. You gave her so many rights that she has begun to reject man's superiority. You are taking away our property, throwing us out and yet you maintain that it is we who are the sinners. Nature settled the worth of woman in these terms:

The wine is his who stretches out his hand and takes it.

But you have endowed wine with equal rights over the wine house. Woman was our plaything. You have exalted her to our status. What an achievement! And yet you don't expect us to even complain! The tyranny of religion has deprived man of his slave and elevated the slave to be seated alongside the master. Now the latest is that a man should not even look at a woman. This compulsory restraint is what you call 'abstinence'. This is your legal convention! I am the victim and I can't complain! This is the condition to which you have elevated women. You have given them rights, whilst depriving men of theirs. I salute this legal skill of yours Sir ... but from afar.'

Had anyone but myself spoken in this way to the maulana, he would have hit him on the head with his staff. But he considers me to have lost my mental equilibrium ... This is why this type of argument often ends on an argument about one or the other of these subjects. I mean that on the day I do get him into too much of a rage, he simply says, 'Idiot, lunatic!' and leaves it at that. But when he gets a bit angry, phrases like—'God forbid!' escape his lips. If the argument is lengthy and disputatious, he gets really furious and thunders, 'Accursed man!' 'Unbeliever!' before the conversation ends. Maulana is a very good man, but has very little good sense.'

29th March 1929

Last night after much solicitation and entreaty, she deigned to pay me a visit. But she was somewhat dejected and sad. I said to her, 'This does not become you, you have been sent to the world to laugh and to make others laugh. What place have tears in these beautiful eyes?' She replied, 'My profession is to laugh and generate laughter but my real self is sad ... Beauty always hides sadness, so does love, although lust has smiling lips and sin manifests itself in gales of laughter!' Sin again! I just cannot believe it. Even she is wrapped up in the thorny issues of sin and virtue. I explained to her until late last night that concepts of sin and virtue are merely the signs of cowardice and laziness in human beings. I said that the framework of life which rests on threats and fear makes a free man servile and indolent. When fear has been imprinted on the human soul, there ceases to be freedom of conscience. This state of affairs is what people call religion. She replied, 'I myself do not set much store by religion but as a matter of form I do say my prayers, and fast from time to time. My complaint against religion is that it has set men above women. You are quite right when you say that where fear is the basis of any arrangement, it drains the humanity of man and makes him passive and helpless. What is the value of those prayers which are offered simply out of fear of hellfire or in the hope of obtaining the delights of paradise? Generally speaking most people are religious in order to impress others or out of fear of disgrace and shame. All such people are either cowards, liars, or steeped in slothfulness, or they are cunning and worldly'... Her glossy black hair was draped over her forehead. Her large arresting eyes were open wider than usual ... she was in this manner courteously explaining the concepts of sin and virtue to me. I said, 'You and I appear to be in agreement so far as the deviousness of imagination is concerned, but what do you mean by saying that religion has set men above women? My complaint with religion is simply that it has snatched from men their rights of ownership and has given women pride of place!' 'Oh, I understand perfectly,' she said. 'Having sucked our blood, you wonder that the bones yet remain. In the name of religion you are lamenting the fact that women are outside your control. In fact your sole disenchantment with religion is that it has given your subjects a few rights and thereby lightened in some degree the shackles which bind them. My complaint with religion is that we are forced to obey its rules, and by so doing are unable to obtain our revenge on your sex in full measure. What a strange situation. We both are alienated from religion, but the causes of our alienation differ. There is disagreement even in accord!' 'In my view,' she continued, 'religion should pass no judgement in the dispute between the sexes. Bring this dispute before Nature's court. Let us not define sin and virtue in terms of the conventions of religion. Come, let us exercise our intellect and our conscience. I will tell you why I consider myself your superior. You are cunning and cowardly. I am neither cunning, nor cowardly. There is much less laziness in me than in you. I carry on a filthy trade but I do not hide my stains nor do I display them as signs of virtue. You are licentious, but out of fear of what people might say, you also resort to trickery and deviousness. I openly sit at home and carry on my trade. But you, when you call me to your house, do so under the cover of darkness, in a closed carriage, and clothe me in a burqa. Then when you sit with me, all the doors of the house are shut. You fear social ostracism and are subservient to social conventions. I am quite independent of such servility. Even religion regards our relationship as sinful. Your sin is in every sense greater than mine because deceit and trickery form a large part of it.'

I can say without exaggeration that this conversation lasted the whole night. She is an extraordinary woman. Her face and attractions arouse my physical passion but her lucid and thoughtful conversation empties my brain of its grey matter. But I am a man. I want a beautiful face. What interest have I in the finer points of philosophy? I am young, wealthy, free and independent. She is only a young girl, beautiful and attractive, who appeals to my sensuality ... I have decided that when we meet in future, I will not allow this type of conversation to come between us ... My whole night has been wasted to no purpose ... How cunning this girl is!

18th April 1929

Akhtar[6], Mahmood, Zaki and Daanish stuck around all day. I had hardly opened my eyes before the whole gang was upon me. Once the gathering began, lunch was consumed in a great hurry. Then they settled down again and did not go until nine at night. I did not notice either sunrise or sunset. Who is a bigger king than I? I have endless time, endless leisure, my only concern being that I

6. Akhtar, Mahmood, Zaki and Daanish are friends of Majnun.

feel hungry four times a day. Come sunrise or sunset, it does not bother me. There is a servant in the house who comes and goes according to his set timings and we have no idea where he comes from or where he goes. Youth, youth, glorious youth! My view is that man should die whilst he is young. The day a man senses weakness or infirmity in his limbs, he should swallow something and sleep forever. The world needs only young men. Old people sit like stones upon the bosom of Mother Earth for no purpose at all. In stud farms, old stallions are shot—why should they go on being fed for free? Such a stud farm should also be established for human beings. All the activities of youth should be fulfilled and when the young men become old they should be put to sleep and buried somewhere. Life is only for youth. Old age is the threshold of death. Upon reaching this threshold, what means does man not employ in order to avoid crossing over it? What stratagems man devises! He takes stimulants and tonics, has monkey glands injected into his system and consumes compounds made of them; he dissolves pearls and precious stones into a solution and drinks it; he wanders around the world in search of some elixir that will give him strength and vitality. What a fool he is! He knows well that death is inevitable, if not today, then tomorrow. But like a rat stuck in a snake's gullet, he seeks to cheat death for a little while longer. Idiot! I have youth on my side, I indulge its pleasures. When I realise that staying awake at night is giving me a headache in the morning, I will know that the fountain of youth is now dry and having collected my worldly belongings, I will summon death with these words, 'Come, I am free, my youth has extracted to the fullest every pleasure in life, the spell of youth is over, I am quite ready, so come. Take me wherever you wish!' In such a manner, and in a spirit of fun I will sleep on a bed of flowers, in the bosom of some beautiful girl. What will happen thereafter? Whatever is to happen, will happen, I couldn't care less!

Maulana Khairuzzaman sits bemoaning the end of all things. What a way to live! Every moment of life you are dying from fear of death. In old age, the fear of dying makes you tremble and you are tormented by worries of Heaven and Hell! I ask you, is that any way to live! You weep in life, you weep in death and bemoan your misfortunes!

22nd April 1929

The young lady is angry with me, and complains that I regard her friends as my rivals. She would like to continue as a fount of abundance for every admirer. She wants to spread her attractions and I am entitled to take my share of them. When she came to visit me day before yesterday, without a sound, I indicated to her that as far as I was concerned, stories of her other admirers did not entrance me at all. It seems that she likes to sit near me and recount stories of the affection and intimacy of other admirers. This activity gives her great pleasure. I told her, 'Please excuse me from having to listen to all this, become intimate with me and leave the memory of other admirers at home.' Then she became furious and said, 'You regard even my admirers as your rivals.' As if they are anything else!

She is a strange woman, and her conversation is even more strange. She lectures me, 'Just be concerned with what concerns you—anything else is not your business. Why should you be jealous of others!' In the same breath she berates the bestiality of men. Had it been any other charmer than Laila, I would have said, 'My dear girl, this arrogance makes a mockery of the beguiling and intriguing ways of beauty. A man will in all circumstances be a man. The tiger does not invite other inhabitants of the forest to share its prey.' It is a tussle for possession between the heart and brute force. But it feels as if I am getting old. As soon as I get angry, I am upset. I get ready for her arrival and say to myself, 'Just let her come, I'll sort her out.' But when she comes, I melt like a wax taper. Sometimes when she begins to say something about herself, how strangely she arches her eyebrows; and a half smile plays around her eyes. She has such an extraordinary way of poking fun at me that I am left speechless. 'So do you mean to tell me,' she asks, 'that you are distressed? You also? Envy is the cause of your distress. After years of sensuality, how did love begin? This unexpected journey from illusion to reality is a most exalted stage in mysticism. But just listen, good Sir. All those with whom you are angry are in the same condition as you. They are dying of love. How many funerals can I conduct? How many can I bury? I am just not capable of digging so many graves. I will purchase the burial ground, and everyone can have his own grave dug.'

On one occasion, my heart is aflame, it says to me, 'The punishment for this woman is that as a sheer gesture of revenge you make her your wife and lock her up in the house ... How much this gilded butterfly prides herself on her coloured wings!' Then when I look up, it is as if someone had struck me across the face and said, 'Shut up, you mannerless fellow.' Then when she goes away, I curse myself. My heart says, 'So this is what you have been reduced to. You who have been the conqueror of a thousand beautiful women! Tales of you as a sensualist and a worshipper of beauty abound! You are in the prime of life. It is your right to conquer any woman who attracts your fancy. Why are you helpless before this woman?' I curse myself and vow that at our next meeting I will really sort this woman out in an appropriate manner. Just let her come this time. I'll be damned if I don't deflate her airs and graces ... I sometimes feel that this woman will not be subdued by the means I have in mind. She is very cunning—the only way is to tie her up in the bonds of marriage. By God! Just let her agree to marry me and all her poetry and philosophy will vanish into thin air .... but the restraints of marriage on my way of life ... God forbid! Has marriage inhibited any man that it should inhibit me? When I get fed up my heart tells me that there is no shortage of women ... four wives are allowed ... and anyway which idiot decrees that marriage also places any moral restraint on a man! Marriage is only the manifestation of the custody of ownership which has been ordained by religious law, similar to the registration of the document evidencing the purchase of property. Payment is either in cash, or there is only promise of payment. This is what is called *meher*.

2nd May 1929

What in heaven's name does this woman want! She is disenchanted by the very word 'love'. She is not a gold-digger; she is irritated by compliments. How cold and dry she is! How I dislike frigid and unresponsive women as partners of sensual intimacy! Every man feels the same way. A man always wants a woman to respond to his passionate overtures. If a woman fails to respond and just keeps sitting in his lap, where is the question of sensuality? An artist's masterpiece or a marble statue is preferable to such a woman. One can happily look at such things and pass time pleasantly. There are so many interests and enjoyments which one can derive from these things. Why on earth should a man sit with a beautiful, lifeless body on his lap? There can be no greater insult for a man than to be unable to arouse any passion in a woman to match his own sensual feelings. What a poor harpist is he who cannot even finger the correct strings to play a tune? Last week she spent two days with me. I asked her repeatedly what the matter was. She kept laughing and in the midst of laughter two tears fell from her eyes. Then she continued to laugh. I am immune to the effects of a woman's tears, in fact in an intimate situation, tears are a sign of lack of pleasure. But those two tears of Laila which I saw falling from her eyes day before yesterday ... I find unforgettable. It is as if they fell from her eyes and into my heart. What on earth has happened to me? God forbid that a woman's tears should leave me in such ferment! This is either old age or cowardice. If this state continues, I can say farewell to enjoying the company of beautiful women!

Akhtar came to see me in the morning. Laila had just left and I was in a wretched state. In any case, Akhtar is always joking, and he then said, 'Are you aware that you have been hooked? And I have a feeling that you have been thoroughly hooked.' At that moment, I also revealed my feelings to him. He then said in a very serious tone, 'I have been watching you ever since Laila started coming and going. Be careful how you proceed. The time has now come to either go forward or to draw back. Analyse your feelings and decide whether it is really just a case of sensual attraction. This is what you have always indulged in or whether your feelings have progressed further. If you have the slightest suspicion that the ground is unsteady beneath your feet, then just retrace your steps. Otherwise, remember, you have had it. Like a hunting dog, a woman's jaw once closed, does not open. All your boasting will ring hollow. If your heart is really distraught over this woman, then marry someone or other. There are beautiful and wealthy girls in your family; you have done plenty of philandering. But this is a serious tangle. Are you listening? Take care that this woman does not make a fool of you and leave you.' God knows what else he babbled. Had I been listening, I would have written it down. It is as if all the equipments of sensual pleasure is being collected for me and a well-intentioned critic has been born. Well, I suppose he also had to appear!

5th May 1929

The danger lies in appearing before her ... in meeting her gaze ... my eyes are my greatest weakness—they allow her a way out! Now she is angry, I too am silent. Perhaps a few days will pass like this and then I will be able to regain my composure ... I am drinking heavily these days, and I keep lots of women around me for company. I laugh raucously all day. I drink heavily and sleep sometime at night in a state of forgetfulness. After getting up in the morning, I have my morning draught of wine, my breakfast, and then my washed-out complexion returns to normal. The lights dance around me again. Are you aware that this is how I try to forget you? In my crowd, no one mentions Laila's name—nor do I ... tongues are powerless to mention that name, but still it dwells in my heart ... when I can bear it no longer, I have a stiff drink ... wreak more cruelty upon me!

11th May 1929

We captured the deer and brought it to the stable to be tied ... but this was not to be ... in one bound the deer broke its bonds and just disappeared. We caught a butterfly in order to cage it ... it fluttered its coloured wings and escaped. A child clamours to touch the moon and hold it in his lap but his outstretched hands remain empty! They cannot reach the moon. Do not rupture the poetry of life—let the deer remain in the forest, that is its home; let the butterfly flutter on the branch of a rosebush ... that is its abode. The moon will remain where it is. Tell the child to clap his hands and dance upon seeing the moon, but not to stretch its hand towards it—it is exalted and remote. I console my heart with the thought that this woman is not suitable for me. Her solemn beauty cannot rival my drunken sensuousness, our sexes differ, our humour does not match, we have assessed each other, and the scales do not balance, then why is there all this vexation? My heart is tempted, my mind tries to explain ... I put my hand on a bottle of wine and swear to forget her ... whenever I am in the throes of wine, youth, sensuality and there is a gap in this sequence, my mind tells me that this discomfiture will last only a few days. I should not worry as I will indeed forget her ...

11th May 1929

An unintended declaration of love ... uninterrupted, unstoppable tears. This is the state of my heart and my feelings are in turmoil! Last night whilst sitting, I went to pieces. How and why that happened I do not know, but my behaviour was childish in the extreme! I am cursing myself; she kept on laughing, I kept on crying. It was just too awful! What had happened to me? She regarded my tormented state with contempt and said, 'At this moment you are not so much a human being as a witless fool. After an age of chasing the physical attractions of women, you have started to pursue love. I am just not prepared to sit all night and witness this breast-beating of yours!'

19th May 1929

I invite her, but she doesn't come. In an admission of defeat, I went there myself. She closed the door. When I sent Mir Sahib, she asked him to tell me, 'When you are in a sensible frame of mind, then I shall come. At the moment, I suggest you sit with a pack of ice on your head for forty days and cool off!'

Akhtar came just now, armed with a load of elegant sermons. God only knows what he kept bleating about. He told me, 'You are a man. You should not allow the superiority of your sex to be so degraded in comparison with any woman, and a shameless woman at that ... a thoroughly cheap woman of no worth ...' I kept on listening, he kept on babbling. At last I spoke. How long could one endure this without irritation? 'I am in a desperate state! I have a greater variety of advice to give than you do. *Mian* Akhtar, I can understand the humiliation which has been inflicted on me by a woman of the street. When she mocks and spurns me, my heart is overcome by a desire to end my life and to end hers ... then when I take control of myself, moisten my lips and clench my fists with the intention of giving a fitting reply to the insults she is heaping on me and on my sex, all at once I feel as if a kind of paralysis both of the soul and of manners has gripped me, I become unable to speak and she says—Are you listening, Akhtar?—she says, "He among you who lays the biggest claim to manliness is the man who proves to be the biggest coward." Do you think that I do not feel these barbs piercing my heart? Every night I swear to myself that after today I will never see Laila's face! And yet in the morning, I am begging her to come the next day. Are you at all able to understand the state I am in? My wits have deserted me ... What has happened Akhtar, even you do not know, and as for me ...'

28th May 1929

My senses which had forsaken me are returning ... experience is but another name for past mistakes. I was trapped in a whirlpool of stupidity, but I have escaped ... my outlook on life came to my rescue. My friends used to wring their hands and shake their heads, saying, 'Oh dear, he is a gone case!' But I still have the capacity to sin within me. Madame Laila sits with a grumpy expression, she is in a bad mood and I have found an escape from love's abyss. You remain exasperated, and I am free. In my life of sensuality and the pursuit of physical attraction, I have been guided by a few philosophical and salutary rules of life which I am setting down in this diary so that my son who is yet unborn can avail of them when he as a young man steps into the world of women and embarks on conquests by following in the footsteps of his *Mujahid* father!

1. A human being should take pride in all his actions and the greater the mixture of sin (as defined by general convention) in such actions, the greater his pride in such actions should be!
2. It is the mind which is the harvest of sin not the heart, or the conscience, and it is the mind which should guide your sensual behaviour.
3. The only difference between an innocent man and a sinful one is that the former clings to a dead and decaying past and cannot break away from its clutches, and the latter keeps heading towards an expanding and challenging future.
4. The spirit of a sensualist is born old, but becomes younger with the passage of time. The more you sin, the younger your spirit will become, although the body is born young and as time passes becomes older and weaker.
5. 'Manners' is a meaningless term. Sensuality in which the spasm of sexual life is present, is real life.
6. A woman is simply a statistic in a man's life. Whether her value rises or falls, depends upon her style of living.

7. The cure for temptation and desire is not restraint, but indulgence.

Many such illuminating guidelines have cleared my way in life. They will do the same for my children and for everyone who reads this diary. Today I said to Akhtar, 'The heat and spasms of sensuality end after a few encounters. I am now again a thinking human being and a ravisher of beauty!' Akhtar was delighted and his face shone with happiness. He said, 'You have escaped my friend but by the skin of your teeth, come let us drink in memory of Laila who is a past episode!'

3rd June 1929

She was so angry with me that she has left this town. Mir Sahib gave me this news. I told him, 'Mir Sahib don't give me news of those who have left, tell me who has come. Have any new goods arrived or has any new establishment been set up? As for women like Laila, they should either be housed in a museum so that visitors can study them, or given a ticket and sent to perform Hajj! In the world of action the existence of such women confounds and distresses those who deserve perfection!

6th June 1929

Life is a name for warmth and movement, the question is whether such warmth and movement should be used sparingly so as to prolong the span of life, or whether by their quick and lavish consumption, the elements of income and expense balance and cancel each other out. Should a flame be kept weak and low so that the light lasts for a long time or turned up high so that there is bright light? The oil which would have lasted for ten nights will be finished in the course of one evening. Which is preferable? The brightness of the light, or the lower flame which lasts for a longer period?

He who is called Allah has tangled human beings in a strange dilemma. In other words the choice is either to grope around in semi-dark corners by keeping the flame low, and by this means, keep breathing for a longer period, or to let the flame burn brightly and for an evening have the whole house ablaze with light and endure darkness for the remaining nights. The oil allotted for each lamp is predetermined. Since the beginning of time a resplendent torch has allotted to each lamp its measure of oil. The more you spend, the less there is. Although, there is an average for expenditure—you can increase or decrease it if you wish. Now tell me if there is no control over departure, and only a certain degree of control over arrival, then what can one do? Either one can expend life's entire potential during one's youth or seek to survive to extreme old age by using such powers in an economical and frugal manner ... the option seems to be that one can either turn one night into day by turning up the flame to its maximum capacity or let it sputter at the lowest level for seventy or eighty years ... one should secure the flame from storms and violent gusts of wind, shelter it in the fold of one's garments, or in some corner niche, in some chandelier, and every day keep checking the level of oil and the wick—now so much light remains ... there is just so much oil ... there is a strong breeze, let there not be a storm, let the oil not fall as that will extinguish the light—one remains apprehensive and in a welter of anxiety but alive. To keep breathing is the main thing ... that should not stop!

When one's house starts to fall into decay, its walls start to sag and cracks appear in its arches, in such circumstances is it not better to demolish it altogether? Or is it desirable to continue to exist in a ruin and keep watching the walls fall down, the roof subside, the column sag, the foundations begin to sink, and to see the slow collapse of the building every day but to resolve that so long as one brick remains standing, one will stay put in that shell of a house, even though one may be crushed when the last wall falls down!

When we reach the stage of life where the decline of youth and the onset of old age begins, there are as many answers to these questions as there are human beings; everyone has his own answer in mind. My view is this—remove the danger of death from life! We are not empowered to remove the condition of extinction from life, had that been the case, we would have done so, but it is not particularly difficult to separate the bitter danger of death from the sweetness of life—you should approach death before it can approach you. Instead of whittling your life away in fear of the danger of death, go towards death without a care, laughing, and in a playful mood! In this way you can save at least half the components of life from thoughts of death's bitterness. Before a band of robbers raids your house, spend all you have and when there is nothing left, open the door and shout, 'Come you robbers, come on. What is there that you want to rob! Grab whatever there is to grab.'

This attitude of mind is that of youth which does not like to be tied to the hard rock of old age and which does not want the dead weight of old age and the possibility of death, tied around its neck. Stay alive so long as you are young and when old age announces its arrival, die all of a sudden. Be extinguished! People understand this point of view but they don't accept it. All these wretched people nourish the delusion that even in old age they can try and succeed in remaining young to some extent. They think that by pouring old wine into new bottles every six months, the wine will cease to be old and become new. They will consume gold and drink elixirs of dissolved jewels, puncture their bodies with needles for stimulants to enter their veins—all so that a woman should not sense any weakening of their embrace. They will insert false teeth into their toothless gums so that their kisses taste the same as those of youth. They will cover their white hair with a layer of hair dye so that even when they are sixty a woman will think them to be not more than forty years old. When one asks their age, instead of telling you that they are fifty, they will always say that they are thirty and will be ashamed even to admit that. They will worry inwardly about age daring to advance without permission. Just as a woman will always worry about revealing her age, so will an old man, who is so busy trying to be young, that he will get anxious when answering any question about his age. This anxiety is acceptable, this embarrassment is acceptable, weakness is acceptable, old age is acceptable, but life is precious ... they would give their life to somehow postpone the approach of death! Death will surely come. It is the only undeniable reality among the realities of life.

I see *Mian* Akhtar in front of me. His countenance is glowing, and there is a victorious smile on his lips. The wretch must have found new prey to hunt last night!

11th June 1929

People say that there was an earthquake at two a.m. this morning, and several shocks were felt. Some old houses in the city fell down, cracks appeared in some recently built walls, and fissures opened up in the arches of some ten or twenty houses, columns became crooked. I learnt from today's paper that in certain places four or five thousand people were killed. One or two citizens have lost everything and are facing ruin. What a shindig has been created over such a trifling matter! It is as if an earthquake is a completely new phenomenon which has never occurred before in human history, an event the likes of which have never before been seen. It is as if yesterday was the first time a wall fell down or an arch developed cracks, or anyone died. The death of four or five thousand people has been turned into an amazing incident which has never before even been imagined.

Early in the morning, Mir Sahib came rushing, 'Oh my dear chap, there was an earthquake last night, what a terrible earthquake it was! I hope you did not—God forbid—feel any tremor?' I laughed at Mir Sahib's confusion and said, 'Earthquake? Earthquakes occur in my life everyday. What's new about it?' Mir Sahib and I had a very interesting conversation. I am writing down what I remember.

Mir Sahib: 'Did you feel any shocks my dear fellow?'

Me: 'Oh yes! Exactly at five minutes past two I was pouring wine into the glass, and there was a shock as a result of which the wine spilt! She was there with me at the time, and she clung to me in a state of shock. When I saw the roof moving, I thought that the rose-coloured wine was stronger than usual, and Mir Sahib, I drained one glass and filled another. I thought to myself that if the roof were to fall on my head, why should I be deprived of one last sip? What do you think Mir Sahib? What else could I do?'

Mir Sahib: 'Dear chap, do stop joking. This is hardly the occasion.'

Me: 'Joke? What joke Mir Sahib? Our conversation is always serious. There was an earthquake—no doubt about that. The danger that my house could fall down and that I could have been crushed to death also has to be voiced, so where is the scope for joking?

She, who was enjoying a moment of intimacy with me, would have also been killed. Had this happened, it would have been preferable to many likely occurrences in the future. I escaped last night, and if I keep on escaping other earthquakes in the future, old age will arrive and my health will start to deteriorate. Too much wine will give me a heavy head, my kidneys will ache, my intestines will start to rot, my liver will be afflicted, I will be laid up in bed for months on end, and will be a guinea pig for doctors, friends like you will have the bother of looking after me, and after all these trials, I will die with difficulty. What is likely to happen ten years hence might as well have happened last night, with a glass of wine in my hand and my arms around my lover's neck. The roof would have fallen in ... and in the morning, all you friends would have pulled out my crushed body out from under a pile of stones and bricks.'

Mir Sahib: 'God forbid, God forbid my dear Sir, you are jesting with death.'

Me: 'I am not joking at all Mir Sahib. The point is that when a traveller has to get to his destination, why should he not take the shortest route? If you have to go from Delhi to Kolkata, why go via Kashmir? You can say what you like, I still maintain that last night a great opportunity was lost.'

Mir Sahib: 'Good heavens, what on earth are you saying! Just think for a minute. A part of the country has been struck by a minor calamity—thousands of children have become orphans, thousands of women widows, and thousands of human beings are homeless!'

Me: 'Mir Sahib, Mir Sahib not so fast, just hold on a minute. You carry on as if something that has never happened or could not happen on earth has occurred all at once. My dear Sir, all children are orphans—you and I are two orphans sitting right here. All women too at sometime or another definitely become widows, houses in the normal course of events, get destroyed.

Then pray tell me what is new? As far as thousands of people becoming homeless and deserving compassion is concerned, my dear Sir, there are millions of people in this world who at any given moment are facing catastrophe. Why should the addition of five or ten thousand to this figure put your spirit in a state of confusion and despair? The parents are to be blamed for their children becoming orphans. Why did they produce the children? Those women who are worried at the thought of widowhood should not get married and those people who are frightened of becoming homeless should not build houses—they should not purchase property or populate towns and cities.' Poor Mir Sahib, hadn't the faintest idea of what I was talking about, and assumed a woebegone expression. When Mir Sahib is unable to reply he starts weeping. 'Mir Sahib,' I said, 'are you aware of the reality which underlies the compassion human beings express? What is it based on? Such compassion is, in reality, an expression of happiness and satisfaction. If you analyse it, you will find a large element of happiness and satisfaction contained in such compassion.' Mir Sahib screwed up his tiny eyes and started to glare at me. 'When anyone expresses sympathy for an unfortunate person, it as if he is comparing his own comfort and leisure with the other person's misfortune. Gloating over the fact that his own circumstances are fine, he says, "How sad that Zaid is so ill!"—he is frightened lest a serious illness strikes him too and is happy that nothing like that has happened. All this sympathy, Mir Sahib, is partly fear and partly selfishness. On seeing somebody die, you say, "How sad that the poor fellow has died", inwardly you are afraid lest death should strike you too. You are thankful that even though death is inevitable—it is just as well that it has spared you for the time being. You are thankful that death has claimed the other fellow and you are still alive. Thank goodness! When you see somebody reduced to beggary and starvation with what compassion you say, "What misfortune has fallen upon this poor chap!" but at the same time you think of the last credit balance remaining in your bank passbook and in your heart silently say, "Thank goodness. I have got enough money. God forbid that I should starve!" Dear Mir Sahib forget all this compassion and sympathy. Those who had to die have died. Those who had to become orphans, are orphaned. When your time and mine comes, we too will go to our grave wrapped up in a shroud. It is possible that we may not even be fortunate enough to obtain a shroud. After all, what is the problem which brings you to my house at this early hour with a pile of newspapers under your arm? My good Sir! Earthquakes occur from dawn to dusk. Is it necessary that whenever there is a tremor, you say it is an earthquake! When I look at a beautiful woman, an earthquake occurs. When your good wife ticks you off there is an earthquake. When on an evening the wine cellar in my house is empty—that is an earthquake. Your old age is not devoid of earthquakes and all my youth is replete with earthquakes—then what do these palpitations of the spirit mean? Why go around weeping? What a shame Mir Sahib that you do not drink, otherwise I would have filled a wine glass to the brim and said:

> *Talk about singers and wine. Don't bother about solving*
> *the secrets of the world.*

... I turned to pick up my box of cigarettes from the small table and when I turned round, Mir Sahib, together with his shoes, had vanished. He must have gone straight to the local mosque and offered *nafil* prayers. He must have sought divine forgiveness, and prayed for my guidance and salvation. Upon thinking of the earthquake, he must have settled down to recite a *wazifah*. I must say Mir Sahib—you really are amazing!

14th July 1929

I spent a month visiting and enjoying the delights of Bombay. I wrote some observations on the city upon pieces of paper, God knows what I have done with them. I have come home quite exhausted. I keep thinking of things as they occur and write them down. There are many matters I have forgotten, but at least let me write down those that I can remember. Anything related to women, I usually do remember, except for *that* woman. Let there be several women and let the memory of one keep being overlaid by the memory of the other. My Bombay visit was hardly educational. However, by that I mean I acquired quite a lot of information about the 'profession' of the flesh trade. From superior establishments where beauty is for sale, to the vulgar market places, and those back alleys which the *shurfa* do not visit during daylight hours, but have no difficulty frequenting at night—everywhere one can either delight in the study and display of a woman's nature, or regard this as a warning. I am concerned with pleasure and keep admonition out of the picture. Even so, I found the attitude to life displayed by this naked and shameless set of Bombay, interesting, because I was new to it all. I witnessed for the first time my name being called out in public. An Indian woman usually waits for the man to make the first move, but the cosmopolitan population of Bombay is different. The women themselves approach men and hail them by saying, 'Hey, where are you going? Come here.' If you happen to pass by close to the doors of their establishments, these women accost you in strange voices and strange tongues. When you enter their boudoir, the terms 'my dear' and 'darling' are lavishly used and as soon as your feet are over the threshold the first question is, 'How much?' Small talk and preliminaries are not allowed. Time is very expensive. There is no time for elaborate and refined gestures—it is all serious action! A client should come in, pay for the goods he wants, and should depart. Frivolity is forbidden! One day I came across a young girl who was somewhat educated. When she started talking in purely commercial terms, I told her, 'Miss Sahiba, I find your business-like attitude rather disgusting. It is interesting and cultured conversation which makes it a delight for a man and a woman to enjoy each other's company. The physical side is only one aspect of the search for companionship. This is not like a paan shop where two paans, no matter how imperfectly prepared, are just swallowed, and thereafter the consumers depart after having had a gulp of water and picked their teeth. The essential condition of pleasure is tranquility and leisure. Even when they are eating, pleasure seekers eat slowly with relish, savouring each mouthful so that the flavour of the food produces a pleasurable sensation on their tongue and the delicious food prolongs their sensuous experience and pleasure for as long as possible. We consider that a woman's company should be as intoxicating for the senses as wine and the effect should last equally long.' When she heard my words, she said, 'What kind of creature are you and which country do you come from? If we wasted time in the pleasures of compaionship, we would starve. People like you are unlikely to put any land or property in our name.' I told her, 'Why are you annoyed Miss Sahiba, don't lose your temper like human beings do, because you are hardly human, you are commercial machines, and machines do not get angry.' 'NO we are not human!' she cried. 'No we are not human. But who has turned us into animals? A shopkeeper displays those wares in his shop which customers demand. If he did not do so, how would the shop run? We display our wares to conform to your bestial tastes. Come to my place one day and watch the fun. See how many big businessmen go there. If absent-mindedly, I start to say a word or two in conversation they get embarrassed and beat a hasty retreat. And you expect social graces! In reality, my purchasers regard me as if I were a tin of cigarettes which they have come to buy. One day I met a Western 'lady'. She told me, 'The occupation which you call love and sensual pleasure in my country has become a part of commercial life. The biggest deals are struck in the shortest possible time!' The real point is time—something which is of no use to man or woman. And how should it be? Everyone is very busy and no one has any time for leisure. In this kind of lifestyle, a time limit has to be allowed for each activity. Otherwise both men and women would starve. I came across another female and asked her, 'Have you ever loved any man?' The poor creature stared at me in amazement. 'Love? I love several men in the course of the day. I dispense "love" to everyone who comes to see me. I embarked upon this profession when I was thirteen years old. I was forced into it. From that time I learned that I should "love" any man who comes to see me for as long as he stays here—whether for ten minutes, two hours, or two months.' 'How stupid you are!' I replied. 'I am not talking about the activity you term "love" I am talking of true love. The genuine thing!' She started laughing and said, 'Does love also have two categories genuine and false?' 'Stupid girl!' I replied. She went on laughing. 'Well Sir, this is something new that I hear—that even love has two categories. The real and the fake! Just as a great deal of my jewellery is fake and just a little is genuine! There are two kinds of love in your country. How amazing, Seth Sahib.' And she laughed even more. I laughed too. What else could I have done? I was embarrassed and also a little ashamed! Then I thought to myself, 'What is it to me? I have not taken up the cause of sympathising with the plight of women. If she doesn't know what love is, it is better that she remains ignorant!'

16th July 1929

One day in Bombay a gentleman came to see me in a state of great agitation. 'Have you heard?' he asked me, 'The astrologers have predicted that according to their calculations another massive earthquake is due to occur on eighteenth. The main thrust of the quake will be towards Bombay. What Sir should we do now?' 'You people have yourselves to blame,' I replied. 'What is the point at this stage of asking for advice?' 'For God's sake,' he said, 'how are we to blame?' 'All the houses that you have built are on the ground,' I replied. 'Isn't that a great fault? If the level of houses had been higher off the ground—say about two yards or so—then you would have had no cause to worry, even if an earthquake were to strike and the ground were to tremble. What pray was the need to build houses glued to the earth?' The poor man thought I had said something profound. He began thinking, but on seeing other people around him smiling, he understood what I meant. 'Well really Sir,' he said, 'what an attitude! Here we are worried to death and you are inclined to joke.'

Life is considered an extremely precious commodity. Life! Although it is something of least value in human existence. What is the price of something which you neither own nor control? Nevertheless, human beings regard 'life' as something which is their own in spite of the fact that we do not know what life is, where it is, where it comes from, or where it goes to. When life is about to depart, you cannot delay it by even an instant! Even then you regard it as being 'yours'. To tell you the truth, the human species is the most stupid species in the universe. Stupid from head to foot! And on top of it, man boasts about being the lord of all creation! He boasts of being the *khalifa* of the world and its governor in spite of the fact that his rule is so weak that he cannot control even one finger of his own hand. There is science, there is medicine, there is genuine and contrived learning, we hear that the atmosphere is being conquered, the mastery of the oceans has been announced, that robots are being made from steel, and electricity is being used to kill dogs and attempts are being made to resurrect them. Someone is resolving to travel to Mars, someone else is concentrating on ways of extending man's natural life ... However, the conquerors of the atmosphere and the oceans, and the travellers to Mars become lifeless in a moment and then lie stretched out on the ground ... lunatics ... fools!

17th July 1929

Last evening *Mian* Akhtar came to see me with a very serious expression on his face. He said, 'Something has to be done ... privately.' Looking at his serious face, I thought he must be bringing news of some new delectable creature. But he had come bearing a new bud of foolishness. He told me, 'My mother feels that I should get married. What do you think?' I replied, 'Forgive me, if your mother had expressed an opinion that she would get married in order to end her widowhood and so that you would no longer be without a father, I would have thought *that* to be more appropriate! But how extraordinary that it should be your wedding that she suggests! A man does not die only once in this world. He dies twice. Half of him dies with the first wound he receives, and the other half with the final wound. Half of him dies when the shackles of marriage are put on his feet. Consider this event to be the end of youth and that of half your life. And the end is also not a happy one! One's wedding night is the start of old age, I mean it is a preparation for the second and final death. And it doesn't end well either! Have you gone mad to be considering marriage in the prime of life! Say to your mother, "If you wish to celebrate my marriage, live a few years longer. Let me reach the age of forty, when my physical powers will begin to decline, when I'll get out of breath just by walking about, or getting up and sitting down—then will be the time to get my *sehra* ready. At the moment, I do not have time for such talk!" Why have you not said this already?' Akhtar replied, 'My mother says that she is longing to see my children, and life is uncertain ...' 'Life uncertain!' I exclaimed. 'Your mother has such a modern attitude. My dear Akhtar, after having spent eighty years in this world, your mother has now realised that life is uncertain! Your mother is no less than the mother of *Luqman* ... Now as to the longing for children, why in God's name don't you tell your mother plainly that there is no shortage of children. Why should you get married just for this reason? Several of your children must be roaming the streets of the town aimlessly. Pick up one, take it home and present him to your mother with the words, "Here mother, here is my child ... the result of the efforts of my youth." Give her a few grandchildren so that she can be involved in bringing them up.' Akhtar said, 'At the moment you are in a typically facetious frame of mind. Let this matter be.' 'This is just not possible,' I replied. 'Since you have brought up the topic, listen. You know my views on marriage. I will now state them, you keep writing them down, and go and show them to your dear mother!'

18th July 1929

Yesterday when Akhtar brought up the subject of marriage and I began to give him a lecture, he tried to run away, but I would not let him do so. I made him sit down, and told him my views at great length—I really gave him an earful. Poor chap! What a dutiful son he is. If Mama says, 'Get married', the obedient son says, 'Very well, Mama!' If Mama says, 'Jump into the lake and drown', or 'eat a little poison', or even 'cut your nose off and dance in the bazaar', even then the son, out of great affection for his mother, will dutifully comply. What a heaven-sent country India is, which has such sons and which produces such scheming mothers!

'*Mian* Akhtar,' I said, 'to get married in the prime of life is to be like a deer which has horseshoes on its hooves, and to get married in old age is to be like a billy goat whose beard is dyed with henna! After all, what is the meaning of marriage? If marriage is simply procreation, then this does not require either a nikah or a *baraat*, and if marriage is to strengthen society, even then it is not limited to the uttering of offer and acceptance. These matters depend on people's outlook. The restraints of marriage are a relic of an ancient era when people used to fight like bulls for one female, and when a woman was also among the necessities of ordinary domestic existence. But now requirements have changed, as has the character of the articles which meet our requirements. Now neither does one go to the bazaar to buy oil nor are lamps used to provide light. An electric wire is fitted around the whole town, and by the mere touch of a switch everyone can fulfil his need for light. Those in a more enlightened society don't even bother to have a kitchen. If they feel hungry, they go out and eat at a hotel. The whole palaver of filling a hookah, freshening the mixture, getting the tobacco to draw, is done away with. There is a box of cigarettes in one's pocket.' So far as the question of children was concerned, I said, 'You fool, when fresh fruit is available in abundance in the market, to go through the hassle of planting an orchard, tending the young trees, and worrying about irrigation is sheer stupidity. In the past, people used to go the river to catch fish. After shivering all day in the winter and getting boiled in the summer, they would bring home one fish to eat at night. Now there are the finest fish already caught and packed in tins, to be bought and eaten at will. If in spite of all this, you still want to sit and doze on the river bank, who could be a bigger fool than you? As to grain or fruit, to produce these is it really necessary to obtain all the rights of zamindari?' I told Akhtar, 'Tell your mother, "Dearest Mama, the problem is that you are a relic of a bygone age. The caravan has moved on. You have been left behind. Now have two meals a day and pass your time. Stay away from the water of a river in which you can't swim."' In truth, this is the great tragedy of human life. Time moves on, people get left behind. Even though they are senior in age, the times are new. Where can they go? What can they do? Nobody understands what they say, nobody recognises them. They are sidelined like fools. They don't understand the new age and when they, without any purpose, try to express their happiness, people laugh at them. These poor old has-beens haven't a clue about why they are being laughed at. I said, 'Akhtar, nikah and the restrictions of marriage are leftovers from the dark ages. Religion and the world are now being freed from this absurdity. Since the Great War[7] the sexual and social relations between men and women are being given a new turn in Russia. There the bonds of family and domestic life are being completely broken and the whole pattern of life is being changed. You are an educated young man and you should realise that in this modern age your mother's existence is entirely and wholly unnecessary. In fact, to an extent, it is a hindrance and it is intrusive. It is by sheer force of circumstance that she is alive and insists on remaining so. But apart from breathing and eating, all her other entitlements have ceased to exist, in this age such parents are like a sixth finger or an appendix—useless but in existence!' 'For God's sake stop this lecture,' replied Akhtar, 'when did I say that I am getting married? I simply said Mama is of the view ...' I stopped him in his tracks.

7. The First World War 1914–1918

'No ifs and buts. I am well aware of the idiotic thoughts swirling around your confused brain. If you are dreaming of the love between husband and wife, remember this—only that husband and wife can remain happy into whose relationship convention has not intruded in the guise of 'love', which is a much abused and debased term. The fact is that the relationship of a man and a woman is only that of pleasure until the ritual of nikah intervenes. If the *qazi* enters through one door to pronounce the nikah, believe me when I say that the pleasures of life fly out of the other door! Nikah and life's pleasures cannot coexist. Life is delightful so long as a woman remains simply a woman and a man simply a man. Neither is she a wife, nor he a husband. But as soon as the words, 'I accept him/her' come in between, perfectly normal decent people shrink into merely becoming husband and wife ... dry, irritable, fractious, ill, and buzzing around with sour expressions.' Akhtar got rather angry and said, 'Babble away, say whatever you want, but I remember just two or three months ago you were dying to get married to Laila. Where was this philosophy and hair-splitting at that time?' 'Temporary insanity is a recognised legal condition,' I replied. 'People commit suicide in this state, they commit murder, they are abusive and violent—all that was a mental frenzy.' 'What a shaky argument you are putting forward,' said Akhtar with a laugh. 'If that was a moment of madness, it can occur again. It will happen again some day. You will bring a wife into your home and I will then salaam you repeatedly.' 'Buzz off you idiot!' I said.

29th July 1929

I recognise the sound of footsteps ... when someone who is desired and longed for wears heels, and they go 'click, click' I can recognise from afar that the sound can either be of Janki Bai or Radha Bai or Zamin Jan[8]! But when the sound of the footsteps is 'clatter, clatter,' then my nerves are bruised and I begin to feel nauseated. *Now he is about to arrive.* I clear the glasses from the table and hide them under the bed. If a female of the house should appear, I tell her, 'My good woman go into the next room and take your *paandaan* with you. His coming has made your presence redundant.'

This is how Maulana Khairruzzaman Sahib arrives. His arrival makes me want to ... how can I describe what I want to do at such a time! He comes coughing, spluttering, and leaving blobs of phlegm in the courtyard and on the staircase, spitting out streams of *peek* and scratching his beard. '*Assalam-o-Alaikum*,' he says. Inevitably his visit begins with the prayer, 'May you be alive and well ...'

Religion, deceit, excuses, force, and dishonesty—whether in the West or the East, have become inseparable elements in our lives and second nature to us. Some aspects have been taught by religion, some by civilisation. But those espousing religion are more to blame because as advocates of truth and purity, they perpetrate deceit and compulsion. '*Assalam-o-Alaikum*' they say and with it add the words 'May the grace and mercy of God be with you'. What they say is absolutely the opposite of what they feel. They greet every Tom, Dick or Harry with the same words, but in their heart of hearts wish that the chap would die or be ruined. Yet their tongue says, 'May you be safe and sound'. Their heart wishes that a bowl of poison be given to the person concerned, yet their tongue says, 'May you have a long life'. In their heart, they would like to tear him to shreds, but their tongue utters, 'May God keep you'. They would dearly like to strip the blighter's flesh from his bones, but the words 'May God preserve you' are on their lips. This is the truth behind the purity of spirit and the sincerity of soul, which in the East is praised by religion and in the West by the guardians of culture. The

8. Courtesans with whom Majnun was involved in the past.

curses in the heart become prayers on the lips and poison is served in the guise of sherbet. This is regarded as the summit of culture. Our Maulana arrives saying *'Assalam-o-Alaikum'* because he needs a donation from me for his madrasah, we say *'Walaikum Salaam'* and shake hands because even now a meaningless fear of religion and the Hereafter still lingers in our hearts.

Our mind tells us religion is merely a deception but our weak heart trembles in case the stories of Heaven and Hell turn out to be true, in case after we die, the windows of Hell should open into our grave. The fools who follow religion blindly are better off than us, as are those who are out-and-out atheists. If nothing else, they attain a degree of consistency. We are suspended in mid-air neither fish nor fowl! The truth is that the inherent simplicity and purity of human life has been so entangled in cobwebs and knots that no matter how many cobwebs you brush aside, even then knots still remain. Every religion teaches morality, but the ability to practise what they preach is very seldom found in religious people. I said '*Walaikum-us-Salaam*' as the maulana arrived, (although in my heart I thought that the fool had descended upon me yet again to waste my time). The maulana came in, sat down, stuffed two or three paans into his month, filled my *ugaaldaan* with phlegm and said, 'Well young man, have you ever studied Islamic history from a psychological point of view?' I replied, 'Yes indeed. I have studied the psychology of the major religions of the world.' 'What difference have you found between the psychology of the Muslims and that of other religions?' 'None at all,' I replied. 'The faults in one nation are, to a greater or lesser extent, present in the others. The manifestations differ, the essence is the same.' 'What on earth are you saying?' he asked in amazement. 'I don't believe you have studied the subject at all. Just consider the teaching of Islam and that of other religions. There is a world of difference.' 'Maybe so,' I replied, 'the terminology differs, the languages differ, the mode of expression differs, but the good and bad qualities are shared by them all, and above all else, they have one thing in common ...' 'And what is that?' he asked. 'The strength and capacity to carry out good work is lacking in them all,' I answered, 'but hypocrisy is present in all religions. The good points are ineffective, the negative points are widespread. Be it the padre, the rabbi, the bishop, the pundit, the maulana—the cloak of deception covers them all. Whatever be in their innermost heart, in practice they are full of dogmatic statements and hypocrisy! My study of their psychology has led me to believe that all purveyors of religions are slaves of their senses. The exception to this rule are those few who forsake the world and seek refuge in some cave in the Himalayas. Even their path is not the correct one. Those secluded mountain cave dwellers are even bigger cowards than the rest of us. They could not cope with the world, so they have run off with their tail between their legs.' The maulana coughed. He always does this before starting an argument. 'My dear fellow,' he said, 'have you then turned into an atheist? Have you become irreligious?' I replied, 'Good Sir, I am neither an atheist nor irreligious. I am a Muslim just like anyone else. The only difference is that they do not say what they think, I state my views openly. I say my prayers on both Eid days in the *Eidgah,* I eat beef, and I am in great sympathy with my community. If in the North Pole, the nose of a fellow Muslim gets frostbite, I begin to sneeze in front of my fireplace! If a Muslim loses his footing in Timbuktu a painful nail sticks out of my shoe. I have every intention before long of awakening the Muslims from their forgetful stupor and of discharging my duty as a Muslim ... let me first discharge the responsibilities of youth. As soon as old age calls, I shall become a national leader, I shall rouse the dead from their graves ... Maulana. I have great noble objectives.'

Then I said, 'Maulana, the envelope is empty. Why bother to stamp it? The horse is dead on its feet, why do you people keep cracking the whip? Somehow or other you have earned your living, just make some personal private gesture whether in the shade of religion or like us long-suffering drunkards. When the time comes, go to where you came from, I don't know where you came from. Just don't bother your head with all these matters.'

The maulana changed the drift of the conversation. 'Have you heard that plague has broken out in the city?' '*Alhamdulillah*,' I replied. 'When every five or seven years the viceroy or the governor visits this area, the town roads are mended and the drains cleaned. In the same way, when every few years plague strikes, arrangements are made for cleaning the town. These are the two reasons why the extent of the town's filth is reduced from time to time. What can I say apart from *Alhamdulillah*?' 'My dear fellow,' replied the maulana, 'what can one talk to you about? Your answers are so perverse. You simply cannot give a straight one. Anyway, tell me, should one be inoculated against plague or not?' 'Respected Maulana,' I replied, 'in this day and age, a crooked answer is the correct one. A straight answer is a sign of foolishness. In any case, you have no need to be inoculated. I do.' 'Why so?' asked the maulana. 'You are over fifty years old,' I replied, 'and I am not yet thirty. The world will be no poorer for your death, but I am capable of carrying on for a bit longer. I am able to fulfil the demands of Nature. Let me remain for a few years more. You go on ahead. Actually neither of us is aware of Nature's mysteries. From time to time by means of calamities, tempests, earthquakes, wars, and disasters she carries out a spring-cleaning exercise, and sweeps away the rubbish entangled in her broom. The sticks and straw lying on the earth cannot compete with Nature. Plague is a very ordinary occurrence. There is nothing to worry about. In fact a few days of fever and painful tumours followed by a swift departure are preferable to all the ailments you will contract by the time you are seventy years old, such as diabetes, gout, asthma, urinary problems—god knows how many other ailments will beset you. You will lie helpless in bed, your family will get worn out taking care of you, your friends will get fed up of having to cheer you up, doctors will get tired of writing prescriptions, and you will depart with great difficulty. When you can travel by express train, or the Toofan Mail why choose a bullock cart!'

At this point, our maulana laughed. I did too. He then began to talk about his children. He loves doing so and by the grace of God, as far as children go, the maulana's arrangements are very well ordered. Every eleven months, the maulana is responsible for an addition to the population of 340 million. The long suffering pious *mullani* cooperates fully with the maulana on this issue. Let's see how long the maulana keeps up this good work!

All the children of the maulana are very attractive. Some are one-eyed, some are dark skinned, some are deaf, some are lame, but the maulana is not at all worried on this score. He knows that after him, they will all be a part of the platform of religious teaching and propagation of religious views. So long as the *jubbah* and *amamah* continue to strike a chord in people's hearts—that is what matters. So what if there is only one eye or one leg? Since when are God's chosen people dependent on transient physical beauty? In his view, the maulana is doing a great service to Islam and that is enough. Finally, the maulana stayed for lunch, and when afterwards I sat with my sitar and asked him if he would like to hear a tune, he departed muttering, 'God forbid'.

19th August 1929

For the past three nights in succession, I was just not in this world of manners, literature, caution, and moderation. In fact I was in a world where moderation is a sin, and where there is neither past nor future. There is beauty, there is sensuality, and there is the present. Today I am lying in bed, trying to shake off my exhaustion. If only sensual indulgence didn't involve exhaustion. My head still aches from the hangover caused by these three nights of drinking. My fancy is poised to take flight. It seems as if there is a woman inside me who is awakening a fresh longing within me. I was just lying down and considering the fact that if even after the Laila episode I am still capable of being lured by physical attraction ... this then may mean that my infatuation with Laila, which at the time I thought was love, was only a sign of the rising tide of my passion ... and nothing more. Was I deceived when I was under the impression that this woman had imprinted the seal of Solomon on my heart and had given to me that thing which brave, generous-hearted spirits call 'love'? Even the most short-sighted, superficial observer in the world will say that my continuing worship of physical beauty is a disorder, which results from my sensual needs. To be attracted to a new woman every fifteen days is from a conventional point of view regarded as unbridled sensuality. But I have resolved this issue in a different way.

That delectable jewel of humanity, that electricity called 'love' exists in the heart of every sensualist and drunkard, and one woman keeps being replaced by another. This means that every woman who savours the embraces of a sensualist for one night or for a few days is a bearer of this current. Then when a man is inclined towards another woman, that electric current is also transferred to the new object of his affections. In this way, the electric current keeps on being transmitted to women in various destinations. Finally it reaches the woman who is being searched for and there it stays permanently. To get to its final destination this current has to traverse many stages. Simply to say that a sensualist is incapable of love and that the women who submit to his embraces are also deprived in this way is just not true. The truth is that this impulse is partly sustained every day by so-called love ... but yes ... that message of love does not form a part of its existence, the impulse keeps passing from one to another until it reaches the last woman—the woman who is sought after and awaited. I do not know who my last woman will be, or whether that last woman is Laila, (What a lovely thought!) towards whom I am again becoming inclined. And it is also possible that this current or impulse of sensuality may all flow into desert sands and finally dry up, or lose its vigour, or stop altogether and this may render that impulse incapable of being transmitted to its final destination! This envelope is still in the post ... it is going from one bag to the other, from one post office to another.

One day I propounded my philosophy of sensuality to Akhtar. He said, 'What an accomplished sinner you are! How clearly you explain and describe your transgressions! It seems to me that this envelope of yours will get lost after being so long in course of post. Some postman will chuck it into a drain and from there it will flow into some cesspit, a sweeper will take it out of the cesspit and mix it into manure. The beams of love will be extinguished in the darkness of old age. Perhaps this impulse or current will just fade out after being transmitted to so many women. Your powder is wet and the fireplace cold!' 'If I stay alive,' he continued, 'I will see the day when you are no longer capable of sinning, you will say, "*Tauba, tauba,*" and you will make some poor, unsuspecting, innocent girl your life partner and it is even possible that your efforts in extreme old age will result in one or two children ... you will sit in a state of drowsiness and like your father and grandfather before you, your drowsiness will gradually become a deep sleep and you will be carried out, borne by four men ... where then will the "current" and the radiance of love be?' 'My dear Akhtar,' I told him, 'you are youthful, and sensual, these things are all good, but you have no taste for the skills involved in these pursuits. That is a pity. As far as you are concerned, human life is a complete and well-ordered system. A man is born, he becomes a youth, he pursues sensuality, and with the onset of old age he repents, he then marries and has one or two children, in his extreme old age he recites "Allah, Allah", and finally dies. You think that apart from these stages, there is nothing else in human life. Although it has to be admitted that in reality human psychology is neither systematically arranged, nor can it ever be so. Human life is composed of and constructed on confusion and disorder. This is not a portrait which can be framed, it does not fit any frame. Nobody's world is similar, there are as many worlds as there are people. Every human being is a world unto himself or herself, one walks about with one's world contained in one's head and heart. Birth and death are the only two things any two people share, and these two events, which are common, are extremely insignificant and mundane just like the first and last blank pages of a book count for purposes of calculation but are not read! If you disregard these two occurrences of life, no one human being shares anything with, or resembles, any other human being from any point of view.' 'Although,' I said, 'emotions, meaning that of lust, love, anger, grief etc. can said to be elements shared by the human species, but if you notice, their processes and manifestations are absolutely different in each case. Every rapture and every situation is completely distinct and separate. Intoxication is quite different from desire. When this is the case, how can you maintain that there is any aspect of human life which is shared and regulated? People write autobiographies, they write biographies, and spell out most of the events of a person's life in one, two, or four hundred pages. Crucially important events in a nation's history are set forth in history books of a few hundred or a few thousand pages ... as if they are lighting lamps to dispel the darkness of past ages with printers' ink and paper. But Akhtar, what is the authenticity of these autobiographies, histories, and biographies? All they do is keep mentioning the obvious things which appear on the outer covers of history. But the turbulence and tumult of human psychology hidden within the covers of history are never penetrated by the thoughts and pens of biographers and historians. Even if you wish to do so, will you be able to delve deep into the tumult of even a single individual's essential existence and reveal all its aspects? Just try this experiment on yourself and on me. Just suppose you wish to write about certain aspects of the life of someone or other—you will then have to devote a volume to each facet—When does that person tell lies? When does that person drink alcohol? When does the person say his or her prayers? When does that person steal? When is that person near a woman? When does that person meets his friends? etc.

Take just one element, for instance, 'When does that person tell lies?' If you have any force in your pen or insight about that person, then start writing the truth. How many lies has the person told? Where, to whom, and why? How many lies has he told as a result of which other people have suffered greatly? How many lies were told merely to cloak his faults? How many pointlessly uttered just from force of habit? How many to gain mastery over a woman? How many to deceive his wife? And how many to mislead his children? On each occasion when that person lied, what were his perceptions, his emotions? How often was he ashamed of having lied? How often were his lies successful, how often not? Your whole life will be spent in writing just one volume. Can you create a well-regulated order in this collection of disorder and tumult which we call 'man'? How aptly, a philosopher poet of Delhi has said:

> *Even as an individual entity, man is a collection of unlimited, tumultuous thoughts,*
> *Although alone, I yet feel myself to be in a crowd.*

People like you keep delving into this unlimited disordered collection; those like me who have some insight into this confusion, pass by with a word and a smile. Why should I waste my time and energy searching for the assembly of others when my own privacy and solitude for me are a multitude? Every human being carries around in his head a similar throng. Who can write the biography of such a person? Who can even reveal one millionth of his life? Let everyone go his own way—you do the same, though do just this much that if on your way you see a pretty woman, explain to her the direction of her (I mean my) house. The point is that my 'light of love' the current recipient of which was with me on the night of the day before yesterday, will very shortly switch affections in another direction!' Laughing, Akhtar left saying, 'Just wait. You and your "light of love". I am going to call Maulana Khairruzzaman Sahib.'

14th August 1929

> *'Sin, become an accomplished sinner, forget the difference between night and day. Enter God's house with a heavy head and a steady gait. Kick the hungry dog from the door, and having belched loud and long, go to sleep on a soft bed.'*

This is a translation of a poem by a Russian poet, which I was reading last night. This unfortunate man has put patriotic sentiments at the end of a poem which began beautifully. He had started to depict all the exhilarations of human life so brilliantly! Every aspect correct and in proportion ... but finally he falls from the sky straight into the dirty pit of patriotism. God in heaven! How aptly had my teacher once told me—a teacher who died poor man; it is often the case that gifted people die early—and how well he had put it! He had said that all the holy men and standard-bearers of religion who proclaim the oneness of God and are enemies of *shirk*, are themselves the worst kind of idol worshippers. They felled the idols in the *ka'aba* and broke the idols of Somnath, but they started worshipping idols which were far more dangerous than those made of earth and stone! Among these are patriotism and love of nation. Man can hide the worst emotions of his existence under the garb of patriotism and love of nation. Those things which from the viewpoint of moral principles are considered undesirable and flawed (I don't accept this code anyway) are hidden under the cover of patriotism. The things I do—the deeds which are undertaken in privacy—all these things and more are done by the patriot in the name of patriotism. I indulge my sensuality, but for the sake of grabbing land and for the sake of ownership I don't cut anyone's throat. He (the patriot) for the sake of a yard of ground marshals columns of troops and slaughters millions of human beings like cattle, or has them slaughtered. I openly flirt with women and I am not ashamed of doing so. He, by making excuses and by fraud and deception, has women widowed and children orphaned, and then he declares himself to be a benefactor and protector of mankind. I indulge in sexual activity with the woman whom I have paid for such services, or without payment, if the woman allows me to do so. But he (the patriot) seizes homes in other nations and then if the conquered call him a brigand, he brings an action of mutiny against such people! I drink and then make love to my beloved. He gives his soldiers drinks and turns them into beasts. His days of delight are very different to my nights of pleasure. Long live the country! May the country endure!

I have never understood why people get taken in by this extremely deceptive double talk. Where there is a pretty woman and a glass of wine close at hand—that is my country. But a patriot considers his country to be the place for the sake of which he seizes other people's women and other people's liquor!

I read a couple of newspapers every day, I read the lengthy reports of cases related to talaq, I read the reviews of films and plays, if there is a story of love, then I read that too, but when in the course of studying the papers, I see a headline related to issues such as—

'Plague in Japan'
'A drop in the gold reserves of America'
'Revolt in Rumania'
'Constitutional government in Spain'
'Resignation of the French Council of Ministers'

—then I just read the headlines and skim through the article. I never waste my time over such rubbish. If the French ministers have submitted their resignation, if there is a revolt in Rumania, or if there is a drop in America's gold reserves, what sin have I committed that I should waste my time and be compelled to read a quarter or half a column about these issues? So long as those of Laila's sex have not resigned from their profession why should I care if prime ministers have resigned in the whole of Europe? So long as distilleries are producing enough whisky, what is it to me if there is a drop in America's gold reserves? As long as there is no disease in India whose poisonous germs are undiagnosed, why should I distress myself by reading about the plague in Japan? Summon all the patriots in the world to compete with me and they will all have to admit defeat. I have very powerful arguments; they are irrefutable, I have rendered even my extremely logical friends speechless. That is the final argument—woman and a decanter of wine. At least these things keep me safe from patriotism, (local or foreign) culture, civilisation, and every other infection of this nature. Woman and a decanter of wine! Had I been writing in place of that foolish Russian poet, I would have ended his poem in this way:

> *'Sin, become an accomplished sinner, forget the difference between night and day. Kick the hungry dog from your door and having belched loud and long, go to sleep on a soft bed. If in the morning, the American flag is planted on the soil of Russia, start drinking beer instead of vodka and if England seizes the place, then drink whisky, if France does so, then drink wine, and if Mahatma Gandhi's spinning wheel starts to spin, drink home-brewed or local liquor and remember—never read newspapers.'*

16th August 1929

Thousands of years ago when man still wandered naked in the forests, when he lived on the trees and in caves—what happy days those were! One day during this stay in the wilderness, a man fell off a high branch into the mud and filth below. His other companions were swinging on the branch and laughed loud and long when they saw him covered in filthy mud. One among them laughed so uncontrollably that he lost his balance and fell in the same way into the filthy mud. He forgot to laugh, he was also hurt. Covered in filthy mud, he got up with a sullen face and walked towards a spring in the forest. He intended to wash himself clean in the spring water, but when he reached the edge of the spring, suddenly he saw his reflection in its clear water. He was covered in muddy dirt, his face was filthy, his arms and legs were covered in mud and a blob of mud stuck to his nose. His whole appearance was comic in the extreme. Seeing his reflection in the water, he started to laugh uncontrollably. Despite his injury, he laughed at his appearance. That was the first time humanity had provided a superb example of manliness—the ability of being able to laugh at one's injuries and sorrows. Even today, thousands of years later, a real man is one who is able to see the comic aspect of distressing and sorrowful things, one who can keep smiling thought his misfortunes and can find an opportunity to laugh at his injuries! This story came to mind because this morning Akhtar said by way of objection, 'You are never serious and go ha-ha hee-hee at the wrong moments.' What had happened was that Akhtar had gone to see one of his lady-loves. He saw his uncle coming towards her door. Seeing this, he had panicked so much that he went into the house. It was dark and there was a takht in the way. He stumbled against it and fell, hurting his nose. In a bad mood he went into another room, but the lady was busy with another admirer. In a filthy mood he came to see me. I started to joke. This made him furious. The truth is that to laugh at the painful consequences of one's own stupidity is very difficult thing to do, and those who are able to do this, have a very high moral stature ... *Mian* Akhtar still has much to learn!

19th August 1929

Nomads ... vagrants ... all are recognised as men and human beings. This world is a wilderness, this life a lengthy road, its beginning and its end are unknown. It is a limitless throng, in which we are travelling, shoving, elbowing trampling, crushing each other, falling over, running or limping along. This is a dilapidated road

... it is called life. Some ingeniously tyrannical creator has made us his playthings ... he has created asses and is playing with them. He pulls someone's ear, or breaks someone's leg, or tweaks someone's tail; some he loads with rocks and stones, others with jewellery. Some people have been fed to bursting point, others who are starving have had food snatched from their mouths. All those asses are running around aimlessly. Where is He? Who is He? Someone has climbed the minaret of a masjid and has started to call. Someone has started to ring bells in a mandir. Someone else has started turning the pages of a book. Arguments have broken out, He is not this, but that, not that but this! God exists in this form, not in that form, and in the midst of arguments some man cried out, 'Is God there? Does He exist?' Then foolish talk started and people fought savagely, the veins on throats swelled, people began to foam at the mouth. What else will dogs eat if not meat? The result? With what result? The same result! People died fighting in this pointless manner ... and after death? Someone said paradise and houris, streams of honey and pools full of milk, someone said strength and salvation, someone else said *awagun* ... None of these fools knows anything at all. Those proclaiming 'Allah Allah' have departed and those shouting 'Ram Ram' have died, either buried in the earth or cremated. Nobody remained, and if there is an Allah, then he remains where he was. Whether you die or are wiped out, cry or sob ... you are not independent, you are under compulsion. In this entire life which is full of more anguish than death, which is hotter than the fires of Hell, the only poetic aspect is woman and the desire which man has for her! But it is unbelievable that those espousing religion want to extinguish even this little ray of sunlight! 'Keep your eyes closed,' they say, 'so that there is no eye contact; don't let your hands touch.' Then there are these threats—hands will be cut off, eyes will be gouged out, the fiery embers of Hell will be forced down your throat.

You will endure the torments of Hell for 70,000 years, will have to bear 70,000 lashes, 70,000 snakes will crawl over your body, 70,000 scorpions will sting you ... I am absolutely fed up with all this coercion and severity. I wish to declare my independence from this contemptible tyrannical system. I want to proclaim that I am nobody's subject, but only a worshipper of eternal beauty and if God is in fact eternal beauty, then I have no objection to His divinity. But my nature will not be repressed by coercion, severity, restriction, and punishment. The worship of beauty is the essence of freedom. Just as a drop confined in a cup becomes free in a river, so my being does not accept being restricted by the confines of religion and wants to remain as free as the flowing river. To whom can I explain my views? To whom can I tell? Fools, the world over, see God in the guise of coercion and severity instead of beauty and kindness. They call these qualities eternal and everlasting, yet they do not regard beauty in these terms ... their heads have been stuck upside down!

25th August 1929

Last night it was very hot in the courtyard and both my companion and I were disturbed by the intense heat. There was no breeze. Both she and I were in a state of intoxication. She said, 'Let us go on the roof and get a breath of air.' Moonlight flooded the place. I picked her up and walked towards the stairs. Her body was in my arms and her fragrant arms were wrapped around my neck. I climbed the first step in one breath like an arrow shot from a firm bow. Her eyes were closed and in my arms she was savouring the pleasure of each step. Having climbed the first flight of stairs, I paused for an instant to strengthen my grip, then I climbed the second flight, at a slower rate, but I was still tipsy. A few fragrant puffs of wind soothed on my face which was flushed with the heat of wine. I also climbed the second flight. Her eyes were shut and her kisses were slowly caressing my neck ... I again held her more firmly my grip and paused for an instant. The third floor was not far; I really wanted to stop on the second floor, but my heart said, 'Let her not think that you are tired.' I again strengthened my resolve and holding her firmly in my arms, climbed the stairs to the third floor. She was quite oblivious to it all but every step was a trial and a difficult one for me. I started to sweat, each of those few stairs felt like a steep flight. My breathing quickened and I began to pause for some minutes after every step. She still had no idea of what I was going through. I was panting and wanted to sit on a stair to get my breath back or put her down. A voice inside me said, 'Don't do this, she'll think you are tired. However tired a man may be, a woman should not suspect this.' Masculine arrogance came to my aid and somehow I climbed the remaining stairs. On reaching the roof. I said, 'Now get down.' She half opened her eyes saying, 'Oh we've arrived already, have we? So soon! Had there been another storey I would have continued to be in your lap like this for a while longer.' The elegance of her 'already' made me feel ashamed. I said. 'There is no further storey, there is the sky. Do you wish me to go towards it?' My heart was asking me when she would get off my lap.... In the open terrace of the third storey I laid her down on a soft carpet. I spread her out like one would the flowers from one's lap, I was bathed in sweat and panting and my back was bent like a bow but she was still intoxicated by the warmth of my embrace. Her heart was beating next to mine in the way a woman's heart beats in a man's embrace. How different was my state to hers! She was deliciously tipsy, I was exhausted. It was as if she was saying, 'Don't stop ... I'd like more' ... and I was feeling ashamed. This is what old age is. The first sign that youth has run its course. When a man cannot even climb three floors with a bunch of flowers in his arms, then consider that the flame of youth has ended. Every man hides this evidence of his decline from a woman. But for how long can he do so? He gets tired, his kisses tire, the grip of his embrace tires, and a voice says to him—

Get up, the delicious dream of dawn is now over.

5th September 1929

Yesterday a friend of Akhtar committed suicide for some reason. Akhtar arrived grief-stricken. He said, 'Suicide is insanity or lack of control or cowardice.' I told him, 'None of these things can explain the philosophy of suicide. Even if you accept that suicide is a manifestation of insanity, even then it is a huge gesture. All great actions result from a state of madness, and none can occur without it. If madness is accepted as the cause of suicide, then undoubtedly this proves what a noble action suicide is. Without insanity and lack of control, there is no difference between an insect and a human being. As regards cowardice, well there is no scope for cowardice in the philosophy of suicide. To take someone else's life, can often be based on cowardly feelings, but to give or take one's own life is the biggest proof of bravery, resolution, independence and freedom. If you focus on the essential meaning of this action, then the decrees of religion and morality and fatwas seem to be nonsensical and meaningless. The highest aspiration of human life is that of freedom, freedom of action, of conscience and of faith upon which religion continues to have a stranglehold. The concepts of coercion and severity have wiped out the glory of God and the meaning of freedom. It is as if man is a helpless crippled leper with a strong rope tied to his nose and like an ox he is pulled by means of this rope. He is made to run, he is pulled along, he is tied up, neither can he take a single step of his own accord, nor can he open his eyes without permission or have a moment to think. Then when one of the oxen takes the ring out of his nose, breaks the rope, and wishes to stake his claim to freedom, he is called an apostate, an unbeliever, and remembered as one who was accursed and rejected.' I read out to Akhtar some sentences written by a famous Russian writer which are uttered by his hero. Regarding suicide the hero argues about his determination and the independence and freedom of man in the following terms:

> *I am amazed by how everyone unhesitatingly goes on living ... in this condition of slavery.... Is there no such being in this world who, as a believer in his personal freedom, is prepared to proclaim his independence by having the courage to take the most crucial step in his existence? I wish to prove my independence and I will do so even if I cannot find a disciple and sharer in my action. I am compelled to shoot myself because to extinguish my life with my own hands is the height of independence!*

Akhtar was grief-stricken for his friend, and was even more involved with his daily whimsical pursuits. He could have hardly understood this point of mine and perhaps he didn't even hear me. He said, 'What is the point of arguing now whether the action of the deceased was good or bad? The grief of having lost my friend is making me desolate!' 'Akhtar,' I said, 'grief has a very shaky foundation. It is simply a meaningless convention. It is an extremely transient condition which overwhelms a weak heart and a feeble mind. The weaker and more feeble the heart and mind, the more this condition takes hold. No grief lasts. If everyone kept count of the instances in his life that had caused him grief, he would be able to remember from the beginning to the end hundreds of such moments which were the cause of extreme anguish and each of those moments of sorrow was such that he at that time considered it to be life consuming. But grief passes and life remains! For instance, when a man's only son died, he bashed his head against the wall, and for weeks, months, and years he was beside himself with grief, his eyes were full of tears and he sat like an attendant at the graveside. Having discarded all the pleasures of life, he was convinced that he would dissolve and die of grief. But what happened? After a short while, he is the same person, the walls are the same, his eyes are dry, the delights of life are the same. Now there is neither candle nor flowers on his son's grave! The grief-stricken father is no longer grief-stricken! He has found several ways of banishing grief. That incident in his life is now like somebody throwing a pebble from the river bank into a flowing river. The pebble makes a plop as it falls into the river; for an instant, circles form on the water, then the surface of the water flows evenly once again. Not for an instant has the current of the river stopped.' I told Akhtar, 'For a start, take the example of your own father. When your mother, his cherished wife, died, for two full years he writhed on the ground and you all thought that he would go mad and die in such a condition! But what happened? The torrent of grief flowed by, and our revered uncle at the age of sixty-five years married again, produced children, and started to dye his beard. He wanders around cheerfully and joyfully with his children in his lap. Who can say that this is the same old man who ten years ago wandered about like a madman in the graveyard beating his head against the gravestones. 'Why on earth' I said, 'should a man allow such a transient and artificial condition to arise in the first place? Why should the pain, which after a short while will certainly vanish, overpower us even for a few days? Why should we allow that to occur at all? Speaking of myself, whenever a dear friend or lover of mine dies, my anxiety and grief last with difficulty until the funeral arrangements are completed. After that, I do not permit myself to be tormented even for a few days by remembering that which is past. I admit that I do have to try a little bit hard to banish this human frailty which is called grief. But believe me I have often been successful in this effort, and in comparison to other people, I have managed to get rid of this weakness to a considerable extent.' 'God forbid that such a day should come,' said Akhtar, 'but if there should ever be such a time, we will also witness your powers of banishing grief.' Then he continued, 'Have you forgotten the state you were in for the love of Laila?' 'You are a fool!' I replied, 'what you call grief was not grief at all but merely a moment of lustfulness, a flash of longing ... if the elixir of love is absolutely sweet, then it loses its intoxication. It should contain a little bitterness. The tears which are shed from the eyes of those who are lovestruck, are an element of love itself. Those tears cannot be compared to the tears which are shed over a shrouded dead body. If you want to shed tears, do so over a living beloved and if I raise any objection, may I be considered a sinner.'

11th September 1929

The love of an attractive woman affects all the vigour of body, mind, and heart, and renders them helpless. However, one's stomach even in these circumstances retains its freedom and independence! No matter how fierce the assault of love, one always feels hungry, and even if not actually hungry, one cannot manage without eating. Whether one feels the pangs of hunger or not, one's stomach has to be paid its dues. One's stomach does not in any way accept the overlordship of love. Those who remember this golden rule make the pursuit of love an easier task for themselves. There was a friend of mine—God grant him salvation—he was six-and-a-half feet tall and a normal chair or bed could not bear his weight, his temperament was poetic, he was of a rakish disposition, by lineage he was a blue-blooded Pathan. He was a landowner and was smitten by a courtesan in Delhi. The period of the year during which he would express his love was fixed. A landowner has to submit dues to the tax collector twice a year—once in July and once in December. These two occasions were the times during which Khan Sahib's[9] passion would be revived. He would collect four or five thousand rupees from his village. He would stuff the amount into tin boxes and go straight to Delhi. 'Love' in all its intensity would begin. Bi Sahiba would also begin exchanging verbal pleasantries with Khan Sahib. For two or three months, day and night, these assignations would continue, Khan Sahib was in such a state that he could not bear his coquettish lover to be out of his sight for an instant. All the while, the contents of the money boxes would gradually dwindle. Finally on a certain a day his servant would announce with folded hands, 'Sir, now only enough cash remains for the train fare home.' The tide of Khan Sahib's passion from being at full flood, would suddenly ebb. His bags would begin to be packed, and a couple of days later, Khan Sahib would depart. Bi Sahiba would come to the station to bid him *Khuda Hafiz*. Khan Sahib would leave for his home ... three or four months later when the money for the kharif crop would begin to come in, the germs of love would begin to be born again in Khan Sahib, and again the same refrain of beauty and passion would start. For almost twenty years Khan Sahib maintained his pursuit of love in this manner, and his companion kept up the relationship. So much so that it was in her lap that

9. The landowner who was enamoured by the courtesan Bi Sahiba

his eyes closed, never to open again! The deceased often used to say that love is unable to compel one's stomach. The mind or the heart are considered as being superior to the body but in matters of beauty and passion both surrender their rules, but the revered stomach does not listen to the commands of love at all. Two square meals a day are essential. Only then can beauty's jeweller test these pearls. The demands of an empty stomach cannot be satisfied by either a full moon or a starry sky. A fistful of wheat is superior to all these things!

19th September 1929

Fools, idiots, racking their brains to no purpose! I am fed up with hearing the words 'Science, Science, Science!' God above knows by what means the lecturer stuffed this devilish concept into my head during my BA course. From that day to this I have never mentioned the word. They say that an increase of knowledge is the reason for the progress of human civilisation and refinement, and that the advancement and expansion of the intellect is the reason for the serenity of man's religious life. Perish the thought! The advancement of knowledge and rational thought has wrecked the world. The progress of rationalism has deprived us of tranquility and spiritual solace. It has divided hearts and minds, and finished forever the tranquility and assurance of life. It has become difficult to breathe because of this advancement of knowledge and promotion of the intellect. Science is now fulfilling the role which religion used to play. In the beginning, religion led to conflicts between man and man; rivers of blood flowed. The sincere and the truthful starved. Just as at long last the hold of religion weakened—lo and behold!—the demon science walks swaggering on to the battlefield. Previously, in the name of God and His Holy Prophet (peace be upon Him) the banners of 'civilisation' and 'morality' were raised, in the shade of which the blood of human beings was drunk and their bones chewed to pieces. Now the demon of science and rationality is imprinted on our minds. There is no place of refuge! Everybody says that science has benefited man enormously, but no one can prove just what the benefit is. If you ask, people say, 'Oh, what do you mean! The railway, the telegram, electricity, the telephone ... the instruments of the air ... this and this and this.' Someone should ask these idiots whether human life was not better before these blessings arrived. Admittedly, journeys took longer and were difficult, food was tasteless, garments coarse and heavy, but how much longer people lived, how much stronger they were, how stout-hearted and confident! It is true that in those days cooks were not so skilled, tailors were not so skilled, the dhobi could not wash clothes so clean without the electric washing machine, but hearts harboured no grudges. Restlessness and weakness also did not exist during that period which today's renowned purveyors of knowledge remember as 'the age of ignorance'.

Man's views on life were simple and straightforward. The star of life was not so fractured as it is at present. This is why hair-splitting is going on about his diet, his confidence and values on the one hand and religious matters on the other. Whilst lengthy sermons are being loudly delivered from the pulpits of cathedrals and mosques, whilst leaders and dictators are singing songs of nationalism and patriotism, human beings are unable to have one meal a day in peace. Compared to 'the age of ignorance', human beings today eat delicious food, but what is the use? The human stomach cannot digest all these delicacies, the beds in which people sleep have a softness previously unknown, but minds are disturbed and nights pass without sleep. Tall towers of knowledge and virtue are being built along the banks of the river of life, but no one appears to notice how dirty the water in the river has become. The quantity of slime and mud is greater than that of clear water! The philosophy of life is stored safely in hundreds of thousands of books with which groaning cupboards are full, but there is less life and more philosophy. A day will come when only philosophy will remain and there will be no trace of life. Man will be reduced to the level of a machine. He will breathe by mathematical calculations, by multiplication and addition. Tubes manufactured in scientific laboratories will be stuffed in his eyes, ears and nose, and his brain will shrouded by the covers of philosophy. Even today, this situation has almost been reached in some madrasahs and institutions of learning where arguments about the following continue to rage and students are embroiled in them:

'Proposition for the completely unknown'
'Concordant precedents'
'Assigning attributes'
'Universal priorities'
'Direct cause'
'Complete or incomplete prohibitions'
'Experimental generalisations'
'Negative delusions'
'Close reasoning or torturous reasoning'

Elsewhere the following are the subjects of argument:

'Additional standards'
'Ondulatory series'
'Knowledge of trilogy'
'Principles of distribution'
'Synthesis and analysis'

While disputes rage on the above, on the one hand ,the lives of students are being wasted over the following:

'Metaphysics'

'Spirituality'
'Self-absorption'
'Personification of the Abstract'
'Beyond Intellectualism'

and on the other hand, there are the following:

'A religion of simile'
'Creative fluency'
'The cylindrical fulcrum'
'Differing critical opinion'
'Collective spirit'
'Emotions lacking force'
'External realities'
'Reaction'
'Self-consciousness'
'Collective consciousness'

Citadels are being constructed and knocked down over the above. There are categories of opacity and transparency and in these rarefied realms, the experts on metaphysics are struggling over implementation—they are by turns constructing and destroying the patterns of their exalted thinking.

These concepts keep crashing into each other. No sooner are they established than they become invalid. Just look at the diabolical length of the list of subjects to be studied. The study of politics, the study of botany, the study of astronomy, of antiquities, economics, sociology, psychology, logic, philosophy, Hindi, the study of triangles, physics, metaphysics, mathematics, geology, and heaven knows what else. There is no limit to the enquiry—and what is the end result? What has been achieved?

The man who does not know and thinks he knows
Remains mired in ignorance until eternity.

The name of this compounded ignorance is culture, civilisation knowledge, and virtue! The technique of words and mental gymnastics! Keep solving and creating the problem!

One day I read an entertaining tale in some magazine. Some respected professor had spent his entire life in calculations and then had come to the conclusion that the world had twenty lakh years of existence left. He had examined the layers of the earth, the variations of climate, the speed at which the earth revolves, and also considered the state of the celestial bodies; he had calculated the decrease and increase in the area of the sea and the dry land and spent all his life embroiled in this misery. Then at last, he reached the conclusion that after twenty lakh years the earth will definitely cease to exist. Upon reading this article, another eminent professor missed one naught, and thought that the former writer was of the opinion that only two lakh years were left in the life of the earth. On this basis, the latter wrote an article in reply and proved that the life of the earth was much more than two lakh years! Thereafter torrential arguments, claims and counter-claims were unleashed in magazines between these two parties, as if the lives of these two professors depended upon the difference between twenty lakhs and two lakhs. These fools have lost sight of the obvious reality that the end of the world will come at the same time as their religious existence ends. It is just a question of five or ten years here or there ... and arguments are continuing about the difference between twenty lakhs and two lakhs!

In the same way, the distance between earth and the heavenly bodies is being measured. Preparations for travel are afoot. The means of communicating with Mars are being invented, as if by establishing a post and telegraph office between the Earth and Mars a great favour is being bestowed on the Earth. Even a journey from the house to the door of the courtyard and from that door to the road is not within one's control, and yet preparations are being made for a journey of five million miles which will take five days!

Have you righted the wrongs of the earth
That you are now hoping to set the skies in order?

Someone should ask these fools whether even if they find out the correct distance between the Earth and Mars, and spend their whole lives in calculation, who will benefit from those useless endeavours? The truth is that our whole life is entangled in technicalities, idioms, perceptions, and concepts. Man's natural and spiritual existence is entangled like a bird in a net. Lofty and magnificent imaginary structures are built, but the foundation of them all rests on the unshakeable reality of the law of destruction. The experts are mesmerised by the science of architecture and they are staring at the sky, they just don't seem to look at the ground. Everyone sticks a label upon his whim. The *jubbah* and the turban have a different label. The sciences and the arts have separate labels—the former does not accept the Gods of the latter and vice versa. Both are drawing conclusions about this world and the next, seated in their respective circles of stupidity. Some conventional attributes have been decided upon, a level of right and wrong has been determined—this is right, that is wrong, this is a sin, that is a virtue, this is correct, that is incorrect, this is pure, that is impure. Why? And where is the proof on which these criteria rest? Forget about any answers to these questions, it a sin even to ask. The staff of the maulana and the pen of the scientific expert are locked in conflict. The victim of all this is the poor fellow who wishes to spend his limited period of life on earth in peace, contentment, and tranquility of spirit, but is not allowed to do so. He is given orders, devoid of any reasons; judgements become binding on him; beyond his understanding and perception, instructions are issued silently without a murmur. Helpless, disappointed human beings are lurching, stumbling, falling, and being dragged along through the dense fog that is their life. They know nothing except that there is no such thing as a choice or an option only unlimited compulsion! 'If your diary was to be published what would happen?' asked Akhtar. 'I'll tell you,' I replied. 'At the most the purveyors of religion and thought will be angry with me. So what if they are? Let them be angry.' If those who are religious deprive me of the blessings of Heaven, and the thinkers put me in a madhouse—what do I lose? Neither have I any desire for the Heaven bestowed by religion, nor do I wish to be admitted into intellectual circles. If these dictators of the world and of religion get angry—what do I care! Let them rage!

28th September 1929

Akhtar read the last entry in the diary with great distaste. 'All these are insane arguments,' he said. 'You close up all the existing options of life and produce none of your own. What do you want?' 'Revered Sir,' I replied, 'How can you change life's realities merely by wishing to do so? You cannot convert a westerly wind into an easterly one, you cannot produce rain clouds if it is not the rainy season—the course is set, and even if it isn't, it is not within our control. The whole of life is beyond our control. You who seek to promulgate rules and regulations for the speed of the wind and the clouds—these are matters beyond anyone's control. Life will go on as it always has. You cannot change the direction of the throng of humanity, the destinations are fixed, the road in some places is smooth, in some places uneven. It is as it is. If you were to say that a fine cemented highway were to be built, that wish would be confined to the length of your tongue. Nothing is going to change. This is precisely why I say don't get involved in these wrangles. Take life as it comes. If it is sunny, you cannot produce shade, when night falls you cannot make the sun come out. You can neither turn night into day nor day into night. In either situation—in any situation—meet it, cope with it, and continue with your life. Conform to the respective demands of youth, manhood, and old age as you reach these different stages, and you don't have to do anything more. Neither thought nor sight, nor complaint, nor reproach, nor longing, nor attempt!'

'These days there is a slump in the beauty market,' said Akhtar with a laugh, 'at least when you are involved in the pursuit of sensuality, you don't talk such rubbish.'

'Choice does not feature in the process of purchase and sale in the market of beauty,' I replied. 'It is compulsion which is the key element. When the time is ripe, only then does a period of sensual attraction begin. It is not possible that someone requests me to become a lover and bowing to the wishes of the beloved, I become a lover forthwith!'

10th October 1929

I see pictures in my dream, as if on a cinema screen past episodes are revived and they become fresh again, the images of the past invade my privacy, I remember forgotten things. Each picture in succession is visible on the screen. I recognise it ... it passes. Who is this? Kamla Devi[10]? What a stunner the wretched woman was! Who is this? Noor Jahan! How wanton and impudent her youth was! This is Mohini!

10. Kamla Devi, Noor Jahan, Mohini, and Anjuman Ara are courtesans of whom Majnun was enamoured in the past.

Those nights in the private garden, by the side of marble pond ... the moonlight reflected on the gentle ripples, the lights of the fountain, and Mohini in my embrace! God knows where she is. This is Anjuman Ara, the brilliant flame of my prime ... how quickly she faded ... resplendent as a butterfly but frail! She paled in an instant like the morning star. Who is this? I can't remember the name, but the face I remember! She was upset with me and left, and then never came back. She is the one who enabled me to forget about the world for two whole years ... an intoxicating glance, enthralling words, fascinating manners, she kept me company for two years and I still remember the delight I felt. There are many such pictures which reveal themselves out of the shadows of my existence, but amidst all these scenes from the past, amidst all this confusion, a picture somewhat hazy also appears. It appears, vanishes, then appears again, and before I can have a proper look, vanishes again.

My eyes blink quickly and repeatedly and they do not have a chance to look at the picture properly, but my heart becomes increasingly restless and says, 'Whoever else it may or may not be, it is *her* picture ... why have I still not been able to forget? .... Why am I unable to forget? If it is *her*—what then? Is that thorn still stuck in my heart? Why do I remember her? She is separate and distinctly visible in the crowd of my past loves, all of whom have receded into the past and been forgotten, though from time to time I recall them, *she* is the only one whom I have been totally unable to forget ... Laila ... Laila ... Laila ...'

12th October 1929

Somebody tells me, 'You must sign a deed, and enter into an agreement. You cannot escape, you cannot avoid this, you are used to making cheap arrangements, but this arrangement is not cheap. It is something else altogether.' In a state of extreme anxiety I say, 'Don't bind me, I cannot sign a deed. I have never done so till now and I shall never do so. I am a man well acquainted in the customs of the flesh trade, she is a sex worker. Both of us are of a kind, we are on the same level, no one is bound to the other, no one is obligated to the other, no one is indebted to the other. This is a commercial transaction, then why do you say, "bring your heart and faith in cash"? What has "heart and faith" got to do with it?'

No one listens, and I am being wrapped in a heavy shroud of forgetfulness, compulsion and helplessness! Where is she? Is she still plying her trade, or in solitude, or in the darkness of the grave? Where is she? I don't want to find out, yet I am impatient for news! I don't want to hear anything, but my ears await the sound. What is to happen? If that is to happen which should not happen, then it will happen at all costs. Very well. So be it. If not to escape is my destiny, so be it. Compulsion exists, but choice does not.

14th October 1929

'Laila' ... 'Laila' .... 'Laila'

19th October 1929

'Laila' ... 'Laila' ... 'Laila'

20th October 1929

Morning: 'Laila'
Evening: 'Laila'
Night: 'Laila'

21st October 1929

Many pages of the diary are empty. A void has opened up in my life. Mir Sahib has brought the news that she is in Benares, and is squandering her beauty with both hands. Benares! The city is taking shape before me already!

... should I invite? ... call her?

... send someone? ... go myself? What is to be done?

28th October 1929

Father, Son, and the Holy Spirit—the Christian Trinity is based on these elements. In the same way other religions too have prescribed pillars. My religion also has three pillars. In Germany Hitler's national emblem is the swastika (the hooked cross). My emblem is a triangle and its three-sided symmetry is made up of the following: beauty, music, and wine.

My world is enclosed within the three sides of the triangle, I keep wandering within these sides and this ambit keeps me intoxicated. The man to whom even one of this trinity is available is fortunate indeed. I swear by my destiny that all three elements are available to me. How difficult it is to give any one of these elements priority over the others! If one of these can be got hold of the other two can be attained. Beauty also brings with it all the intoxication of wine and the exhilaration of music. Wine is often accompanied by beauty and music. Music arrives with beauty and wine hidden in its robes. Who is the unfortunate being who wishes to go beyond this trinity apart from our revered Maulvi Khairuzzaman?

That man is a flawed jewel who only worships beauty and is indifferent to music, or who drinks wine but is not a worshipper of beauty. Life is only fulfilled when the three sides meet and the triangle is complete.

9th November 1929

When I am agitated by love's complications, when I am fed up with life's struggles, when I am irked by the very name of religion and find the restraints of law and morality loathsome, the thought sometimes occurs to me that man's most natural religion in the world is the 'religion of suspicion'. Why should awareness of this religion not be spread all over the world? This religion has been propagated under different names in earlier times. Past ages, however, were not conducive to the complete success of this religion ... but now ... the difference between reason and religion has produced an atmosphere which is extremely suitable for the propagation of the 'religion of suspicion'. There is no reason why I myself should not take the field as the founder and prophet of this religion and invite existing and future generations to embrace this religion. In every religion that has appeared on earth so far, Satan's strength has prevailed over the strength of the Almighty. No religion can claim that it has annihilated or exhausted *shaitaniat*. In fact, history shows us that in the life of religious nations *Ahraman* had many more subjects than *Yazdaan*. The fact of the matter is that religion itself has conceived *Ahraman* and Satan as extremely powerful and until the day of judgement, their strength will be imposed upon mankind. After having done this, religions have exhorted their adherents to 'fight against this foe ... confront it, defeat and crush it; this is the path of virtue'. The 'religion of suspicion' will be entirely free from the old sectarianism of religion, it will abolish entirely the difference between *Ahraman* and *Yazdaan* and will base its teaching on the previous worthless truths of man's religious life. The adherents of this 'religion of suspicion' will be free from any system or discipline because system and discipline themselves are the cause of the greatest deficiency. This 'religion of suspicion' will define life in the following terms: Life is complete confusion, incapable of cure. Do not regard anything as an article of faith, do not believe anything, the good and bad qualities of things and people are merely conventional terms and unreliable. Regard with suspicion whatever comes in front of you, lay down neither rule nor exception for life, do not accept any rule or any exception thereto, acceptance and acknowledgement of a retraction is in the 'religion of suspicion' the worst and extreme form of blasphemy. Remain as free, as innocent, and as unaware as you were born. Search and enquiry is a crime, discernment is a sin, comply with your natural instincts, keep clear of the absurdities of intellect and understanding. People make claims of being a prophet but they are not free of religion's ancient concepts; they present the same amorphous substance in different guises to the world and in some form or another present the concept of *Ahraman* and *Yazdaan* to the world. All this is wrong, I don't want to make any hasty claim of being a prophet, I am about to present to the world a state of affairs where any semblance of order and arrangement has ceased to exist and total chaos reigns. I am making preparations to ensure that arrangement and order have no place in my prophetic message. I wish to place before the world only a few vital principles which will change the lives of my *ummatt* and deliver them from a false sense of balance into complete chaos—that complete chaos which is the most undeniable of all life's realities!

Last night I said to Mir Sahib, 'After a few days, I am about to declare my prophethood.' The poor man was so stunned his face fell a mile. Stroking his straggly beard he said, 'Heaven forbid my dear fellow. Today you are decided on prophethood. Tomorrow you will claim divinity!' 'Mir Sahib' I said, 'I will make you the first among the number of adherents of the "religion of suspicion". Those people who set themselves up as being too religious are the very people who are more susceptible to conversion and blasphemy. Their minor blasphemy is more severe than the major blasphemy of an apostate.' Poor Mir Sahib after listening to these introductory strictures got up and went to say his *Isha'a* prayers!

11th December 1929

I have opened this diary after one and a half months. I spent this period in Benares, the time went by without my knowing it. When did I return? Why did I return? How did this time pass? Akhtar and Mir Sahib are present here with me and tell me that I was extremely ill. My condition was critical. The doctors had given up, my friends were in despair ... I say all this is wrong.... When Laila spent forty-five days and forty-five nights at my bedside, when her hands moistened my parched lips with water, when her fingers clasped my pulse, and her dulcet voice filled my heart and soul with tranquility—in these circumstances, who can dare to presume that I was ill? The truth is that never in my life have I been so healthy as I was during the past one and a half months. Though my temperature was hovering around 105 and 106 degrees, the fire of life had never blazed so fiercely within me. My spirit was never so full of vigour. These blind people think that I was ill! It is only now that my illness is beginning, when my bedside is lonely and my nurse has gone! Her words were, 'You were a stranger in this city, you came to meet me, you were my guest, I merely fulfilled the duties of a host. Now go back home, so that I can occupy myself in my professional activities.' 'Why this poison after the sweetness of honey?' I asked. 'You were helpless and therefore deserved my attention,' said she. 'Now you are no longer sick, so now go home, and if you want to avail of my services come and see me like any other customer.'

I am sick of the taunts of Mir Sahib and Akhtar. Day in and day out they let loose poisoned barbs at me. 'Enough. The Turkish is over. A brave man has surrendered! He has unbuckled his sword! This is also how the heads of the brave lie in the dust. This is the way in which great riders are trampled beneath the hooves of their horses.' Do things always happen in this way? If you spit on the sky it falls back on your face! The claims of victory are wiped out in this shameful defeat. Enough! I shall say no more, just lie on my bed counting the joints on the ceiling!

13th December 1929

Yesterday I again sent a proposal of marriage. I also received my answer. 'If it is my destiny to marry you,' she said, 'I don't need to say yes, what is to happen, will happen. But as opinion, pleasure, and permission have also been involved in our relationship, I will die but I will not say yes. No, No, No.'

Then she told Mir Sahib, 'Tell him that our beautiful and poetic relationship should not be sullied by the dry, unappealing, and turgid concept of marriage. Why do you wish to leave me with an insipid and tasteless memory? If you imprison the colourful butterflies and the bulbuls, the colour will come off the wings of the butterflies and the songs will be stilled.

You, who want religion to put the stamp of approval upon your sensuality, do you think I am such a fool as yourself that I should sacrifice my poetic and aesthetic feelings to the dictates of religion? If you love me, do so, but then why the urge for ownership? When I was afraid that your longings might make me a captive, I ran away, but now that you have come here with the same old proposal, I am not in the least bit afraid of your longings. You want an answer. My answer is that you go home and obtain the hand of a decent, innocent girl and ask Mir Sahib to say *ijab* and *qubool*. She will be your legal mistress and your chattel. You will be her lord and master without the involvement of any outsider! The poor creature who has spent fourteen or twenty years within the four walls of her house as a slave to her parents' wishes, will be fairly satisfied in your prison, because she has never tasted freedom. She has only known one aspect of life, and is happy with it. What does she know—poor innocent creature—that a world exists beyond this captivity, where women do not fall prey to man's beastly tricks, where a woman is not recognised as someone's wife, daughter, sister, or mother, but as a separate individual in her own right, free from the snares of men and also enjoys an exalted stature!' Then she said to Mir Sahib, 'Tell him on my behalf—love me as ardently as you wish, but please have mercy on me and don't take the handcuffs and chains out of your pocket, and offer them to me as jewellery. You take out the handcuff and chains from your pocket, and when you do so I can see the burning fires of Hell, when I am in your embrace I wish to run away and you follow me bearing those chains. It will be difficult to catch me like this as the world is very wide, my wings are very strong, and to this day no man has dared to lay his hands on them! So long as you desire me, I shall enjoy the delights of your desire to the fullest, but when you come towards me bearing the weapon of nikah then I will spit with contempt upon the ground and move on. You and your proposals of marriage! You claim to love me and send me proposals of marriage! What has love to do with marriage?' 'Tell him,' she said with a laugh to Mir Sahib, 'that either you are an absolute idiot, or an extremely cunning rascal!'

15th December 1929

The titles of idiot and rascal are being conferred on me. 'You don't even acknowledge religion,' she said. 'Why then do you seek to interpose religion between us? What kind of jest is this that the same thing applied to you is deadly poison, but for me pure honey?' When I think about the matter, something does seem to be amiss. Why is it that Laila's footstep at once shatters my philosophy of life and scatters it in confusion? Is it that like a crafty man I want to promulgate such a law for women which can in no way apply to me? I cannot bear to give to a woman the freedom and rights which I give to myself. I want the regulations and centre of her life to be dictated by me. Either all this is true or the fact is that my longing has made me so helpless and I have lost my senses to such an extent that I want to make this woman mine whether in accordance with my own rules of faith or otherwise. But she is aware of the flaws in my arguments and my logic—a man doesn't even want to allow this right to a woman! When a man is in the grip of sensuality, he says that this is all there is to life; but when I am subject to the emotion of love, I say that I have no principle and no faith, because I am a lover. She laughs and makes a face. I then get angry at love and then resort to sensuality. To stoke my sensual feelings, I discard all serious religious principles, but when sensuality tires me then it is subdued by love. At that time, I think of new arguments and new issues and let those horses gallop in the field of love. She claps her hands and laughs, I weep and beat my breast. Sometimes some friend says, 'Take a decision!' I also agree and ask myself, 'Why don't I decide?' But at the very thought of taking a decision both 'sensuality' and 'love' are unhappy. Both tell me that there is no such species as 'decision' in their realm. So long as I am accompanied by 'decision' I cannot enter the realm of either. I am being swept between these two deities. It is as if a current is sweeping me along, towards the valleys of the hills, towards fields, and into the bosom of the desert, towards forests, the shade of oases, and the sweltering wilderness. How long will this state of affairs continue? Where will this current take me—and in which level of the ocean will I be deposited? I think of such things and then I get angry at myself for doing so, then again I start thinking. Sensuality, sensuality, love, love ... if only a way could be found between these states, if only a door would open which would be separate from both of them. Sometimes I am reminded of these lines of a foreign poet:

In the dark night ... a child cries for the light.

19th December 1929

'Come home,' says Akhtar, 'start thinking straight, and tighten the loose screws in your brain. To be so impatient for a woman is incompatible with manliness. If a tiger were to weep for the love of a lamb then he would starve to death.' The example of the tiger and the lamb, goes to my heart. I say to myself, 'I'll go to Laila's doorstep and there humiliate the entire race of womankind, and say, 'Look, you hard-hearted and insolvent wretch and see what a man is like!' In the next instant all these resolutions melt into thin air and at length I lie down and then have to endure Akhtar's small stabs for the whole day. Last night Akhtar produced a woman from Benares or somewhere else. She was very coquettish, playful, and sharp-tongued, with sparkling eyes, restless hands and feet, and sharply etched eyebrows. She made herself entirely at home—sometimes she was in my lap, sometimes I was in hers, the wretch gave me so much to drink that I was not in my senses. Half the night went by without my knowing where I was. Countless stories were heard and told about the powers of beauty, the victories of love. She told me about her lovers, I told her my tales. 'Tell me,' she said, 'who did you love most of all?' 'Laila,' I replied, 'but now I loathe her.' 'If you loathe her then you are a liar,' she replied, 'you could never have loved her?' 'I loved her as no man has ever loved,' I said, 'but she did not value my feelings.' 'She saw through you,' replied the woman '... every woman can recognise a hollow drum.' 'She is shallow,' I replied. 'It is not she but you who are shallow,' said the woman. 'You have seen your face in her mirror.' In this way matters progressed, and the drinking session continued.

'I want to burn her up, and humiliate her,' I said. 'I want to show her that women more beautiful than her are available to me.' 'Come,' I said to her, 'Let's go to Laila's house. You can talk to her and I can lessen my anguish.' I thought that the woman would never agree but she agreed! We both at once went to Laila's house, and had the door opened with difficulty. Laila had gone to bed. She sat up upon seeing me. I took the woman from Benares by hand and introduced her to Laila. 'Forgive us Laila, the two of us wished to take the air and wanted to drop in and see you on the way.' Laila smiled, 'Please be seated,' she said. My eyes became brighter, my heart happier. 'I wish you had brought some of the cool night air for me,' said Laila, 'it is extremely humid.' Having introduced the two women, I lay down. I thought let's see how these two butterflies go for each other. Laila talked about this and that. My odd behaviour had no visible effect upon her countenance. As was her custom, an undying smile played on her lips such as I have to this day never seen appear on anyone's lips. A riot of merriment sparkled in her eyes, and her tone was mischievous. Of the effect I wanted to create, there was not the slightest indication. I closed my eyes in disappointment. 'You are sleepy,' said Laila, 'go to sleep and I will rest in another room.' So saying, she put her hand on my shoulder. I was quite drunk, and the touch of her hand sent a current through my body, 'No,' I said, 'I'll be going.' But my legs failed me and I sat down again. 'I will not allow you both to go,' said Laila. 'Fortunately, my bed is unoccupied this evening.' She smiled and said, 'Both of you go and rest.' After this I said something, I don't remember what it was. She then said something. Goodness knows what. When I woke up in the morning, I found myself in Laila's bed. The woman from Benares was asleep beside me. Her warm breath wafted against my hair and swirled round the room. I sat up in confusion and cried, 'Laila! Laila!'. Akhtar opened the door of the room; 'Where is she?' I asked. Akhtar said, 'She's gone away. She left this morning before I arrived. A servant and some of her luggage remains. Her servant says she's gone to Bombay—God only knows. She has left a note for you. 'How amateur last night's performance was,' she wrote, 'but I am happy. Don't allow the poetry in your life to be snuffed out. Keep performing. Don't worry about any storms which may break upon this rock of life—

swing on swings, play in the gardens—just don't think. Remain free from thought and worry. Thought is a message of death. Don't think about anything. This is the prescription I myself follow. Even before yesterday, I had decided to go to Benares, I didn't think it right to disturb your sleep. This world is very confined, and so I am sure that one day you and I will meet again ... we cannot get lost ... farewell!'

Epilogue

Last night, I slew the being
Who used to sit within me,
Who used to frighten me, threaten me,
Who constantly picked at my heart
Sometimes saying, 'Don't do this—this is a sin'
Sometimes saying, 'Do this—this is a virtuous act.'
Sometimes saying, 'You will go to Hell'
Sometimes saying, 'Make yourself worthy of Heaven'
The being who used to taunt and disturb my sensuality,
The being who made me restless with constant barbs,
Sometimes reminding me of Heaven, sometimes of Hell
Sometimes regaling me with tales of the spirit, of God, of death,
Stories ... false, absurd, meaningless tales!
Last night I killed that ill-mannered being
And went confidently to sleep.
In the morning I put my hand on my breast
Thinking that now that I had killed the being, there would be an empty place,
Lo and behold! The being was still there.
The same wretch! The being said,
'Fool! Every night that you kill me
I will be alive the next morning, seated in my abode of peace
Every day, every morning, you will find me here where I am.'
Religion ... civilisation ... animals!
Now can somebody tell me what I should do?

Glossary

Ahraman: Personification of evil, a concept of ancient Persia.

Alhamdullilah: 'God be praised.'

ammamah: A turban worn by Muslim divines.

angarkha: A masculine dress of the nobility of eighteenth century Avadh.

Assalam-o-Alaikum: Muslim greeting meaning 'peace be unto you'.

awagun: Transmigration of souls.

ayat: A verse of the Holy Quran.

azan: The Muslim call to prayer given five times a day.

baraat: A wedding party.

batasha: A round white sweet made from dissolved sugar.

burqa: A garment worn by Muslim women covering their face and body.

churidar: A tightly fitting pyjama with folds around the ankles.

Daagh: A famous Urdu poet of Delhi of the late nineteenth century.

Eid: Two major Muslim festivals. Eid-ul-Fitr marks the end of the month of Ramzan. Eid-ul-Azha marks the completion of the Hajj and commemorates Abraham's sacrifice of his son Ismail.

Eidgah: A place where prayers on the occasion of the two Eids are held.

Farhad: A stone cutter in Persia who fell in love with Shirin, a most beautiful woman, and committed suicide in the mistaken belief that she had died. Farhad and Shirin are symbols of love similar to Heer and Ranjha.

fatwa: A Muslim religious decree which though without legal force can be regarded by sectarian believers as binding on the basis of sectarian religious convictions.

fiqh: Islamic jurisprudence.

ghazal: A love poem in rhyming couplets.

Gulzar: An Urdu poet, probably a contemporary of Qazi Abdul Ghaffar, who wrote in the early twentieth century.

Hadith: A tradition, a narration of a saying or action of the Holy Prophet (peace be upon Him).

hakim: A doctor, a practitioner of the Unani system of medicine.

houri: The status in the Hereafter of women who are decent and pious their earthly life. They will become chaste inhabitants of Paradise.

ikkah: A conveyance drawn by one horse, a one horse carriage.

isha'a: The Muslim prayer recited in the evening.

jihad: A struggle, a war waged by Muslims in defence of their religion.

jubba: A robe or gown; a long coat.

ka'aba: The House of Allah known in Arabic as 'Baitullah' in Mecca which Muslims pilgrims circumambulate during the Hajj and Umrah ritual.

kheer: A sweet dish of rice cooked in milk—a kind of milk pudding.

khalifa: A successor to the Holy Prophet (peace be upon Him).

khichdi: A savoury dish made of split pulse and rice boiled together.

Khuda Hafiz: Words of farewell used by Muslims meaning 'God have you in his care'.

Laila: The celebrated beloved of the legendary Arab lover Quaisbin Omar. The name Laila is a classical symbol of the beloved.

Lota: A vessel for holding water.

Luqman: A famous teller of fables. A wise man.

madrasah: A school, college academy or seminary for imparting religious education.

Majnun: The name given to Laila's beloved—Quais bin Omar.

masjid: A mosque, a Muslim place of worship.

masnavi: A long narrative love poem.

matab: Consulting room of a Hakim, where he sees patients.

meher: Financial settlement made by a Muslim husband on his wife at the time of marriage.

mehrab: An arch, whether of a mosque or other building a feature of Islamic architecture.

minar: The minaret of a mosque or other tower—for example, the Qutub Minar in Delhi.

maulana: A little of respect given to a person for their learning.

maulvi: A Muslim divine.

mufti: Title given to a learned Muslim.

murid: A disciple.

Maulana Shaukat Ali: Brother of Maulana Mohammad Ali, a Muslim political figure in the early twentieth century who was reputed to be robust.

Munkir: One of the two angels who will cross-question the dead in the grave.

muezzin: The person who gives the call to prayer from the mosque.

nafil: The optional element of Muslim prayer.

nikah: The Muslim ceremony of marriage.

Nakir: One of the two angels (the other being Munkir) who will cross question the dead in the grave.

para: One of the thirty equal parts of the Holy Qura'an.

paandaan: A receptacle for keeping the betel leaf or paan.

peek: The juice of paan, the betel leaf commonly chewed in India.

purdah: A veil, a cover, refers to the seclusion of Muslim women.

qazi: A Muslim legal official who amongst other duties, solemnises Muslim marriages.

qismat: Destiny, fate.

Qutub: The Qutub Minar (or tower), a famous architectural landmark of Delhi.

sarod: A stringed musical instrument used in classical Indian music.

sarangi: An Indian musical instrument.

sehra: The floral face-covering worn by a bridegroom prior to the performance of the marriage ceremony.

shirk: Belief in the plurality of God.

sikanjabin: Fresh lime juice cordial.

sitar: An Indian musical instrument used mainly in Hindustani music.

sherbet: A non alcoholic drink, syrup.

shaitaniat: Devilry, evil.

Shariat: The code of laws in Islam which Muslims regard as being divinely ordained.

Shurfa: (Plural of Sharif) persons of high rank and family.

takht: A low seat, a bed.

talaq: Divorce under Muslim law.

tola: A weight of gold.

tasbih: A string of beads, a rosary used by Muslims.

taweez: An amulet, a talisman.

tibb: An indigenous system of medicine.

Tilism-e-Hoshruba: An Urdu epic; the title literally means 'The Magic Which Bewitches the Senses' which was part of the literary tradition of Avadh.

Ugaaldaan: A spittoon.

Ummatt: The word refers to a religious community, generally used to refer to Muslims.

Valima: The function (usually a banquet) which evidences the consummation of marriage.

Wazifah: A daily or routine recital of a religious incantation

Zamzam: The stream which arose out of the desert when the infant Ismaiul, the son of Ibrahim cried for water. The stream continues to this day and is regarded as a miracle.

Zunnar: A distinctive belt or girdle, part of the clothing that Christians in Jerusalem were required to wear to differentiate themselves from Muslims.